John : Witness and Theologian

JOHN
Witness and Theologian

JOHN PAINTER

Foreword by C. K. Barrett

LONDON
SPCK

First published in 1975
by SPCK
Holy Trinity Church
Marylebone Road
London NW1 4DU

Printed in Great Britain by
Northumberland Press Limited
Gateshead

SBN 281 02879 6 (paper)
SBN 281 02880 x (cased)

To my parents

Contents

Foreword

Serious study of the Fourth Gospel becomes more difficult as the years pass. The generation that has elapsed since the end of the Second World War has witnessed the discovery of fresh materials which in themselves are sufficient to justify more than a lifetime's study. Almost at the same time, in 1947, there were discovered the first manuscripts from the caves of Qumran, and the Coptic Gnostic library of Nag-Hammadi. In the view of many, these two archaeological discoveries frame the Gospel, the former shedding new light on the background from which it emerged, the latter illustrating the Christian Gnosticism to which it made a fundamental contribution. During the same period the resources for the textual criticism of the Gospel have been enriched by (to name one example only) Bodmer Papyrus II (P^{66}), which contains most of the Gospel and dates from about A.D. 200. Anyone who wishes to understand the Gospel in its historical context must be aware of all this material, and anyone who wishes to make a contribution to the study of the Gospel may be expected to have mastered at least some part of it.

During the same period the output of modern studies of the Fourth Gospel has been immense. Probably no one has read it all; I know I have not. Rudolf Bultmann's great commentary was already complete before 1945, but it did not become generally known outside central Europe till the war was over, and the English translation did not appear till 1971. Also in the post-war period the lifework of C. H. Dodd appeared in *The Interpretation of the Fourth Gospel* (1953) and *Historical Tradition in the Fourth Gospel* (1963). Here was an approach different in many ways from Dr Bultmann's, yet, like his, leading to a profound theological apprehension of the meaning of the Gospel. Meanwhile another leading German scholar, Rudolf Schnackenburg, was at work on what promises to be the biggest commentary of all, of which so far one volume, containing an introduction and commentary on chapters 1—4, has appeared in English translation (1968). America has not been idle, and Raymond E. Brown, in two volumes of the Anchor Bible (1966, 1970) has given a most valuable survey of a generation's work and added his own very important insights. The English reader also has before him the somewhat smaller but hardly less important commentaries of R. H. Lightfoot (1956), J. Marsh (1968), J. N. Sanders and B. A. Mastin (1968), and B. Lindars (1972), together with monographs, large and small, such as Aileen Guilding's *The Fourth Gospel and Jewish Worship* (1960), M. F. Wiles's *The Spiritual Gospel* (1960), E. M. Sidebottom's *The Christ of the Fourth Gospel* (1961), P. Borgen's *Bread from Heaven* (1965), W. A. Meeks's *The Prophet-King* (1967), E. Käsemann's *The Testament of Jesus* (English translation 1968), and J. L. Martyn's *History and Theology in the Fourth Gospel* (1968). I deliberately confine myself to works of outstanding importance that are available to those who read no language but English, and omit articles, which are innumerable, and the classical works of earlier generations.

The average reader may well feel that Johannine studies have got beyond him. He certainly has no time, and may lack inclination or even ability, to read all even of the major works. He needs a guide, who himself knows the literature, ancient and modern, and has thought through Johannine problems with an independent but sympathetic mind. It is a pleasure to me to have the privilege of introducing Dr John Painter as such a guide. Of his qualifications for this role I can speak with first-hand knowledge. After earlier studies and some parish experience in Australia, Dr Painter came to Durham as a research student in 1965, and for some years we worked together on the Fourth Gospel. He is now Associate Professor at Cape Town University. He has professional knowledge of the subject and experience, spread over three continents, in explaining it to students and others.

The reader will see that Dr Painter introduces the Gospel in its historical setting with great brevity. Doubtless he would have been glad if space had permitted him to go into the problems, and the many hypothetical reconstructions they have evoked, in more detail. I have given, however, some hints that may show how complex these problems are, and it is a virtue in Dr Painter's book (which is not a history book) that he so quickly gets to grips with what is likely to be of most concern to most readers—the theology of the Gospel (and of 1 John too). There are a few points in his exposition about which (as he well knows) I should wish to argue with him, but it is brief, comprehensive, scholarly, and helpful, and thus manifests a set of virtues not often seen in combination. Many readers will be grateful for it, as I am myself, and I wish him and his book well.

Durham
March 1974

C. K. BARRETT

Author's Preface

I have written *John: Witness and Theologian* with the conviction that the time has come to restate the theology of the Gospel and First Epistle of John. The progress of Johannine studies (especially in the light of archaeological discoveries) has produced what is commonly called 'the new look of the Fourth Gospel' and of 1 John as well. A systematic presentation and assessment of the theology of the 'new look' has been urgently needed, especially for students. Much of the material has been available only in journals and specialized monographs. Now I have presented the material in one volume in such a way as to make it accessible to all who are seriously interested. The book, based on careful study, is not intended for the experts only. It is intended primarily for students and for the serious reader.

Of course the views expressed are my own. But the major alternatives have been outlined within the limits of available space. I consider my views as an expression of the 'new look', either in terms of general agreement, or because they arise out of its insights. Discussion of the various views has made it necessary to insert detailed material which breaks into the exposition of Johannine theology. These insertions outline the various views or indicate the basis of a particular interpretation or set out the implications of a specific view. These sections are indented to distinguish them from the exposition and may be omitted without breaking the argument. But the student will find much invaluable material in these sections.

A bibliography has been added as a guide for further study. This is not intended to be an exhaustive list of the works available. It is specifically restricted to books that are available in English and an attempt has been made to indicate the more concise works as well as the major scholarly contributions. Thus the bibliography is designed as a guide to further reading rather than as an indication of the works out of which this book has arisen. For those who are interested, attention is drawn to more extensive bibliographies.

Now that the time has come to let this book go I have to restrain the impulse to revise it yet again, aware that a book is never finished. It has to be abandoned! Not that I wish to change the views expressed, but I would like to have expressed them more adequately to do justice to those who have made the whole enterprise possible. D. W. B. Robinson (now Bishop Robinson) must be held responsible for my interest in New Testament Studies. St John's College, Durham, made the basic research possible. Professor C. K. Barrett turned my attention to St John. He and Mrs Barrett have been unstinting in their friendship and encouragement to carry this work through to a conclusion. The final form of the book has been produced in Cape Town with the encouragement of Professor J. S. Cumpsty. I wish also to acknowledge those who have assisted with typing and the reading of proofs. Throughout the years my wife Gillian has supported the endeavours which, in part, have come to fruition in this book.

Cape Town
March 1975

JOHN PAINTER

PART ONE
Introduction

1 *The Author*

It is a maddening fact that the author of the Fourth Gospel has given no clear indication of his identity. What he has written is sufficient to indicate that he was one of the most profound thinkers (theologians) in the early Church. It is this, as much as anything, that presses us to discover who wrote the Fourth Gospel. The answer that we give to this question could affect the way we understand the Gospel.

If there is no clear indication of the author's identity, how did tradition come to ascribe authorship to John the apostle? About A.D. 180 Irenaeus, Bishop of Lyons in Gaul, wrote his great work against the heresies of his day. In this he identifies John the apostle with the beloved disciple (mentioned in the Fourth Gospel) and indicates that he was the author of the Gospel and Epistles of John as well as the Apocalypse (Revelation). His knowledge of this tradition was apparently dependent on 'the elders' in Asia Minor, of whom Polycarp and Papias are named.

A strange silence surrounds the earlier history of the Fourth Gospel. The first clear evidence of its existence is in Gnostic (heretical) circles. Because of this association it might have been rejected by the Church but for the strong advocacy of Irenaeus. He claimed that, rightly understood, the Gospel was a weapon to be used against the Gnostics. With the tradition of Johannine authorship, we have to take account of this shroud of mystery that surrounds the Gospel. Added to this is the fact that the testimony of Irenaeus has been impugned by many modern scholars because certain statements are in conflict with what is said by Eusebius, the fourth-century Church historian. This conflict raises questions about the accuracy of the testimony of Irenaeus.

Bishop Westcott marshalled the internal evidence to show that the author was a Jew of Palestine, an eye-witness, John the apostle. In this narrowing down, Westcott took the evidence of chapter 21 at its face value. But today most scholars regard chapter 21 as an addition of doubtful value with regard to the evidence of authorship. Only here is the anonymity of the Gospel set aside and the beloved disciple is identified as the author. If this evidence could be taken at face value, it would seem that the cryptic description referred to John, identifying him as the author of the Gospel. But there is no scholarly agreement at this point. Some identify Lazarus as the disciple Jesus loved, in chapters 1 to 20, and claim that the addition of chapter 21 has confused the issue. There the disciple is identified as the author and intended to be recognized as John. Others claim that this disciple is an ideal figure, maintaining the anonymity of the Gospel.

The evidence is not unambiguous, but the addition of chapter 21 was intended to indicate the identity of the author. The external evidence, including that of the Gnostics and the tradition stemming from Irenaeus, attests Johannine authorship. But how are we to account for the lack of information about the Gospel until the second part of the second century? What are we to make of the corporate editorial notes in chapter 21? Many scholars also draw attention to a number of breaks of continuity in the text of the Gospel. How are these to be explained?

One way around these difficulties is to see John as the origin of the tradition which was ultimately expressed in the Gospel. Around him a school of disciples developed and the Gospel ultimately issued from them. This theory has many possible variations. In general terms it provides a working hypothesis. It takes account of the claims that the Gospel is based on eyewitness testimony (1.14; 19.35; 21.24) and explains the late appearance and doubtful acceptance of the Gospel in the second century.

2 *The Readers*

It is important to realize that the books of the New Testament were written with specific readers in mind. We understand the books best when we have some understanding of the readers. Is John a Gospel for Greeks, reflecting a Greek background?

While C. H. Dodd recognizes a merging of Greek and Hebrew thought, he considers that it is the Greek sense which predominates in the Gospel. This presupposed background has a bearing on the interpretation of the Gospel, especially concerning Jesus as the Logos and the meaning of truth. This has clear implications concerning the purpose of the Gospel. It is understood as a missionary tract for 'higher pagans'.

Rudolf Bultmann is critical of Dodd's presupposed Greek background. He interprets the Gospel against a Gnostic background. Recognizing the syncretistic nature of Gnosticism (it borrowed its garb from many and varied sources), he argues that this mythology presents a unified understanding of existence new to its time. It recounts, with many variations, the fate of the soul. It tells of its origin in the world of light, of its tragic fall and imprisonment in the body, of its deliverance and return to the world of light. Each soul is a splinter of light from the world of light. The splinters are released through the coming of the Revealer, disguised with a body in order to overcome the demons. He awakened 'his own' and taught them the way of return to the world of light.

> Bultmann thinks that the evangelist was originally a disciple of John the Baptist, who in reality was the founder of a Gnostic sect (Gnostic Baptist sect). The opening verses of the Gospel (the Prologue) originally celebrated the incarnation of the Logos in John the Baptist. When the evangelist became a Christian he applied the hymn to Jesus. The hymn was only a small part of the source material drawn on by the evangelist.
>
> 1. There was a 'Signs-source' (John describes the miracles of Jesus as signs) containing much of the narrative material.
>
> 2. There was the Passion-source, containing much of chapters 18—20, which may have been attached to the Signs-source.
>
> 3. There was the Sayings-source (Revelation discourses) which included the hymn now used in the Prologue and much of the sayings material. These sayings originated in the Gnostic Baptist sect but the evangelist used them as sayings of Jesus. Used as such the sayings have become an anti-Baptist polemic. But this source theory has not been widely accepted.

According to Bultmann, the idea of the incarnation is an expression of the Gnostic myth and is to be reinterpreted as an assertion that Jesus is the Revealer. He is the man who opens up the true meaning of existence to other men. He brings a new self-understanding to men.

Since the discovery of the Qumran texts many scholars have emphasized the Jewish character of the Gospel. In terms of style and the expression of a particular form of dualism the Johannine writings resemble the Qumran texts more closely than any other contemporary body of writings. While there is no evidence of John's dependence on Qumran, the texts do seem to indicate that the milieu of the Johannine writings was Palestinian Judaism, at least in origin. With the Qumran texts the Gospel manifests a dependence on Old Testament ways of thinking. But the strong emphasis on knowledge and the dualistic development set them apart from the Old Testament as manifestations of Judaism in the Hellenistic age.

The concentration on knowing in John is greater than elsewhere in the New Testament. The two Greek verbs meaning 'to know' are used over one hundred and forty times (more than the total use in the Synoptic Gospels). John shares this emphasis with the Qumran texts. But the most important comparison is the dualism. Both in John and at Qumran this was expressed by the use of antitheses, light and darkness, truth and falsehood, flesh and Spirit, freedom and bondage, life and death, love and hate. The conflict rages between good and evil, between the prince of light and the prince of this world. In the conflict men are called to the crisis of decision, to choose the light or the darkness. (The dualism of the Qumran texts is expressed in a classical passage in the Rule of the Community (1 QS 3.13—4.26).

Both in John and at Qumran the dualism is modified by the biblical doctrine of creation (1 QS 11.11 and John 1.3). The dualism is used to indicate that men are called to decide for the light or the darkness. It has been described as 'decision dualism', the decision involving allegiance to or the rejection of the sect. At Qumran this involved acceptance of the sect's interpretation of the Law and in John an acceptance of the person and role of Jesus. Thus the dualism is used to express the conflicts within Judaism.

3 *The Nature of the Gospel*

What kind of book is the Gospel of John? It is a profound interpretation of the gospel events. But it is not true to say that John gives a developed theology while the other Gospels give us the gospel history. We need to take account of the theology of the Synoptics and the historical content of John. Each of the evangelists was a theologian in his own right. In John theological reflection has progressed beyond the limits of the Synoptics. It has reached a stage where the sources can no longer be detected with any certainty. Discourse and narrative are expressed in the same style and bear the impress of the mind of the evangelist. In spite of this monolithic unity, almost all of the important Johannine themes can be found, in seed form, in the Synoptics.

John develops isolated sayings into major themes, for example concerning 'the new Temple', 'new birth', 'eternal life', the faith of discipleship, the person and work of Christ. But John's use of language differs from the Synoptics. The kingdom of God, so central in the Synoptics, is mentioned only in John 3.3,5. This is because his main emphasis is on the complementary themes of the person and work of Christ and the experience of salvation. Because of this perspective, John ranks with Paul as one of the leading theologians of the New Testament. It is the genuis of John that he gave expression to his theology in the form of a Gospel. But, unlike Mark, John does not refer to his book as a Gospel. In fact he does not use gospel terminology at all. His book certainly is a Gospel. But where does the gospel tradition end and where does faith take over the theme? What is the relation between history and theology in John?

Totally objective historical writing is not possible. Event and interpretation are inextricably bound together because bare events are meaningless. Events only have meaning when they are understood in a context. Thus events may be understood in different ways. The event remains unchanged, but it is understood from different perspectives. This point is crucial for understanding the nature of the Gospel of John.

John is a Gospel. It contains a historical account of the ministry, death and resurrection of Jesus and presents these events as good news. But, unlike the Synoptics, John does not appear to be a collection of traditional material, edited and fitted together. John exhibits a freedom of composition. This statement needs to be balanced by John's strong emphasis on witness.

> Witness terms are used 47 times in John and only 6 times in the Synoptics, 4 of which refer to the false witnesses at the trial of Jesus. This terminology is used in the strict sense of giving firsthand evidence.

The Gospel records the manifold witness to Jesus and for this reason can itself be described as witness. But the author also claims to bear witness to what he has seen with his own eyes (1.14; 19.35; 21.24f. and also 1 John 1.1ff.). The historical nature of what was seen is indicated by the use of the Greek aorist tense in 1.14 (we saw) as well as by the terminology of witness.

Understanding the Gospel is complicated by the fact that it has been written from the standpoint of two different perspectives. Time and again the Gospel presents a profound understanding of the person of Jesus and then indicates that the disciples failed to understand his significance. This is because the Gospel was written from the perspective of faith, which issued from the glorification of Jesus, but it describes the situation of Jesus' ministry. The Gospel operates at two levels. There is the level of understanding that was possible in the days of Jesus' ministry and that which was possible after his glorification.

Jesus' glorification and the coming of the Paraclete are related events. Together they were instrumental in bringing a renewed understanding of old events (2.22; 12.16; 7.37ff.; 16.7,13–16). As a witness, John retains the perspective of the disciples' failure to understand Jesus, but at the same time he indicates that the record of the same events, which were misunderstood by the disciples, can now evoke authentic faith. Thus, while showing what the words and works of Jesus mean for faith, he continues to emphasize the misunderstanding Jesus encountered.

Misunderstanding is a recurring motif in the Gospel. Not only the disciples, but also almost every person or group coming in contact with Jesus is shown to have misunderstood his words and works. The misunderstanding motif has its roots in history. Jesus was misunderstood. Misunderstanding arose because Jesus was thought of in traditional Messianic terms.

> The misunderstanding motif in John should be compared with the Messianic secret in Mark. In Mark, Jesus silences those who would confess his Messiahship openly. It was suggested that this was a device to cover the fact that Jesus did not claim to be Messiah. But it is more likely that this is an indication of Jesus' rejection of the Messianic role as it was then understood in Judaism.

The misunderstanding motif also illustrates a theological point. Jesus' glorification and the coming of the Paraclete were necessary events to bring about true understanding. But perhaps the pedagogical function is even more important. Why did John bother to record Jesus' words if they were always misunderstood? He records Jesus' words and works with the response of misunderstanding in order to remove the misunderstandings which persisted in an age when authentic understanding had become possible.

4 *The Structure of the Gospel*

C. H. Dodd has outlined the structure of the Gospel attractively.

A. Proem: Prologue and Testimony	1.1–51	
B. The Book of Signs	2.1—12.50	
1. The New Beginning	2.1—4.42	One miracle
2. The Life-giving Word	4.46—5.47	Two miracles
3. The Bread of Life	6.1–71	Two miracles
4. Light and Life	7.1—8.59	No miracles
5. Judgement by the Light	9.1—10.39	One miracle
6. The Victory of life over death	11.1–53	One miracle
7. Life through Death	12.1–36	No miracles
Epilogue to the Book of Signs	12.37–50	
C. The Book of the Passion	13.1—20.31	
1. The Farewell Discourses	13.1—17.26	
2. The Passion Narrative	18.1—20.31	
D. Appendix	21.1–25	

But this analysis is not altogether convincing.

There is no good reason for separating the latter part of chapter 1 from what follows. All of this could well be described as witness or testimony.

The title, the Book of Signs (2.1—12.50), overlooks 20.30 and the possibility that the resurrection of Jesus was the greatest of the signs. 20.30 seems to suggest post-resurrection signs.

The sevenfold arrangement of the Book of Signs is forced. While Dodd recognizes that, in John, 'sign' involves miracle, in his analysis of the seven signs some include two miracles, others one miracle and two of the signs include no miracles. John refers to many miraculous signs and records seven in detail. From these accounts it is clear that a sign is a miracle with a meaning. The signs were intended to lead men to faith (20.30–31). Their function becomes even clearer when it is noted that Jesus does not refer to his miracles as signs, nor is sign a particularly Johannine word. (It is used seventeen times in John and thirteen times in Matthew.) It is the word used to describe the miracles from the standpoint of the onlookers. Jesus described his miracles as 'works'. This description is characteristically Johannine, and there it is found only on the lips of Jesus. (In John the noun and the verb 'to work' are used thirty-four times, whereas they are only used a total of sixteen times in the Synoptics.)

The miracles, which others call signs, are referred to by Jesus as his works. The works fit into the scheme of witness to Jesus, and the Gospel is best understood as a Book of Witness. Witness is concentrated in chapters 1—12 (Jesus' public ministry), but is not restricted to this section. The witness to Jesus (where the actual terminology of witness is used) can be listed as follows:

1. The Baptist (1.7,8,15,32,34; 3.26; 5.33)
2. The Woman of Samaria (4.39)
3. Jesus (5.31; 8.18; 18.37)
4. Jesus' works (5.36; 10.25)
5. The Father (5.37; 8.18)
6. The Scriptures (5.39ff.)
7. The crowd (12.17)
8. The Paraclete (15.26)
9. The Apostles (15.27)
10. The 'beloved disciple' (19.35; 21.24)

The whole Gospel contains witness, but there is a concentration in chapters 1—12 because these chapters deal with Jesus' public ministry. In these chapters the world is confronted with the complex network of witnesses and challenged to believe in Jesus. The theme of witness continues in what follows because the Gospel is to be witness to Jesus for subsequent generations. The place and effectiveness of this witness is outlined in chapters 14—17 and 20. Paradoxically, it also becomes clear that the witness that produced only a superficial faith during Jesus' life-time is capable of provoking authentic faith in subsequent generations.

The repetitive character of the Gospel has been noted frequently. There is a lack of development in this Gospel. From the beginning the full significance of Jesus' person and work is revealed. Each new incident follows a similar pattern. The pattern is determined by John's understanding of the nature of revelation and the response which it provokes. Bound up with this is the pedagogical use of the misunderstanding motif.

The pattern can be stated in general terms. By his words and actions (particularly his signs) Jesus drew attention to himself, revealed himself. This revelation always met with a mixed response, it caused division. Rejection of Jesus is to be seen alongside the acceptance of him as a prophet or even Messiah. For those who accepted him in these terms Jesus had further revelation. This revelation draws attention to the misunderstanding involved in the Jewish categories and goes on to clarify the significance of Jesus. The pattern is concentrated in chapters 1—12, but it is also to be found in chapter 14. It was not only unbelievers who misunderstood Jesus. The believers also needed to have their view of Jesus corrected in order that their faith might become authentic.

The Gospel is a Book of Witness to Jesus.

A. Prologue (1.1–18) introducing all main themes including witness.
B. Public Ministry (1.19—12.50).
C. Private Ministry (13.1—17.26).
D. Passion Narrative (18.1—19.42).
E. Resurrection appearances and conclusion (20.1–31).
F. Appendix (21.1–25).

5 *The Purpose of the Gospel*

The purpose of the Gospel is clearly stated in 20.31, or is it? In general terms it is clear that the Gospel was written to promote believing. But is it to promote believing for the first time, or going on in faith? Both views have their advocates and can be given support from the Gospel. The context of 20.31 and the recurring pattern that we have noted indicate that we are faced with a false alternative.

John wrote to promote authentic active faith in Jesus. Active faith is expressed by John's invariable use of the verb 'to believe', never the noun 'faith'. The use of the verb is often clumsy in English and the noun 'faith' (understood actively) is more appropriate. Authentic faith is indicated by the content of faith in 20.31, believing that Jesus is the Christ, the Son of God, believing in his name. These designations are clarified through the pattern of revelation and response, misunderstanding and correction.

The nature of the misunderstanding informs the reader concerning the situation in which the Gospel was shaped. The basis for the rejection of Jesus was the understanding of the Law in the Judaism of Jesus' day. His opponents were 'the Jews'. Even those who believed Jesus misunderstood him in terms of expectations within Judaism. Clarification always occurs in the context of Jewish misunderstanding. Thus 'Christ' (Messiah) and 'Son of God' are reinterpreted in the Gospel. The Gospel was written to promote this reinterpretation.

> The Jewish character of the Gospel has been confirmed by the detailed comparison with the Qumran texts. The texts provide us with evidence of Hellenistic influence on the Judaism of Jesus' day. Hellenism was directed by a spirit of universalism, but its impact on Judaism was divisive. Sectarian Judaism was a product of the Hellenistic age (the age inaugurated by the conquests of Alexander the Great), even though some tendencies in this direction can be detected earlier.

The Judaism which forms the background of the Gospel was

fragmented, the Sect of the Way being the most important division. Because these divisions threatened the life and faith of Judaism, pressure was brought to bear on all 'heretics', especially Jewish Christians.

> About A.D. 85 'The Test Benediction' (*Birkath haminim*) was published to provide a basis for excluding heretics from the synagogue. One clause was designed to exclude Jewish Christians. In the New Testament only John uses the technical description for excommunication from the synagogue (9.22,34); 12.42; 16.2). Confession of faith in Jesus was sufficient ground for excommunication, which would have lasted as long as 'the error' persisted. This measure was designed to discourage converts from belief in Jesus and it achieved its aim reasonably well (12.42). The problem of the ostracism of Jewish Christians became apparent in the time of Paul. Because John shows no awareness of a formal test, it would seem that the formation of the Gospel took place before A.D. 85.

The threat of excommunication encouraged Jewish believers to keep their faith secret in order to stay within the fold of Judaism. The case of Nicodemus is treated as typical (3.1ff.; 7.50ff.; 19.38ff.).

> The repetition of man and signs in 2:23–25 and 3.1–2 links these two passages together. Nicodemus is the typical man who believed on the basis of signs. He is also the typical ruler who would not confess his faith openly because of excommunication (12.42). He is treated as one of many who kept their faith in Jesus secret. Secrecy because of fear of the Jews is even typical of the disciples (20.19).

The threat of excommunication was also used to make timid believers recant. In John 9 the parents of the man who had been blind were so intimidated that they refused to acknowledge how their son had received his sight. But the man who had been blind overcame intimidation and was excommunicated because he refused to reject Jesus. He became the model of the true believer in the Jewish situation.

This was the situation confronted during the formation of the Gospel. It raised the question, which the Gospel answers, 'Why does believing in Jesus necessitate breaking from Judaism?' If the choice is Jesus or Judaism, can it be shown that the choice should be for Jesus and against Judaism?

John sets out to show that the revelation in Jesus justifies facing persecution. He presents this revelation as the fulfilment and abolition of Judaism.

> The Prologue asserts that the revelation in the incarnate Word superseded the Law of Moses (1.17f.). The Old Testament, like the Baptist, is rightly understood only in terms of its witness to Jesus (1.7,8,15,32,34; 3.26; 5.33, 39,46f.; 8,56,58; 12.41). The Jews' religion had given place to a superior way (2.1–11). The contrast is not between water and wine, but between poor and good wine. The best was kept until last, compare Mark 2.22. The Temple had become obsolete and the risen Christ has become the New Temple for the meeting of God and man (2.13–22; cf. 1.14). The identification of the kingdom of God with Judaism is denied (3.1–15). Those who believe in Jesus enter the kingdom. National boundaries are broken down so that all who believe in Jesus receive the Spirit and are the true worshippers of God (4.23–24; cf. 7.37ff. and 1.12f.).

The Gospel was formed for Jewish Christians to clarify the significance of Jesus and the meaning of faith in him so that believers would be encouraged to make an open confession of faith. Such a confession would lead to a confrontation and ultimately a break with Judaism, as inevitably as it did with Paul. Rejection by the Jews would have led to mission to the gentiles. As demonstrated by C. H. Dodd, the Johannine language would have had a strong attraction for intellectual or pseudo-intellectual pagans.

The publication of the Gospel reflects this new stage and presupposes the presence of gentiles. While the composition of the material occurred in a situation of conflict between Jewish Christians and Judaism, the publication of the Gospel took place after gentiles had joined the community. Thus Jewish names and customs are explained for their sake (1.38,41; 2.6,13; 5.1; 6.4; 7.2; 11.55; 19.31,40). These statements about 'Jewish festivals' also reminded Jewish Christians that the festivals were Jewish and not Christian. The name 'Christ' is interpreted for gentile readers, but in the Jewish sense of 'Messiah', not as a personal name or in the Gnostic sense confronted in 1 John. These explanations were probably added with the editorial appendix (chapter 21) when the Gospel was published.

> It is worth noting that the movement from Jewish to gentile situations had taken place by the time 1 John was written. In this new situation the Gospel might well have been used as a missionary tract. If so it was misunderstood, and 1 John was a necessary response to clarify the situation. The misunderstanding suggests that this was not the purpose for which the Gospel was written. It is a theology of mission, not a missionary tract. Its purpose was to provoke the Church to the kind of faith which is expressed in mission, not to provide an apologetic approach to intellectual pagans.

APPENDED NOTE ON GNOSTICISM

The term 'Gnostic' needs some clarification. British scholars tend to restrict the use of this title to describe the widespread manifestation of heresies in the second century A.D. German scholars are inclined to use the title more inclusively of a pervasive movement which, they claim, antedates and influenced the development of primitive Christianity. It is used in this sense by Rudolf Bultmann. In his commentary on the Johannine Epistles, C. H. Dodd also used the title in the broader sense, drawing parallels from the second-century heretical literature to fill out the position of the opponents in 1 John. But Dodd later rejected this broader use (in his *Interpretation of the Fourth Gospel*), probably because of the tendency to read back all of the characteristics of the later movements into the earlier manifestations. This tendency overlooks the contribution that Johannine Christianity (and Pauline also) probably made to the fully developed Gnostic mythology, especially with regard to the myth of the descending and ascending redeemer. But the broader use has the merit of drawing attention to the similarities between the earlier and later manifestations. Thus when 'Gnostic' is used of the opponents of the author of 1 John it does not imply the fully developed mythology including the descending and ascending redeemer, except where the views of other scholars (e.g. Bultmann) are being discussed.

PART TWO
The Theology of the Gospel of John

1 *Symbolism in the Gospel*

The presuppositions of this exposition have now been outlined. The Gospel is best interpreted against the background of Judaism. The author was a Jew steeped in the Jewish tradition. But he was also a Christian who was vividly aware that his own people had rejected the Messiah whose coming the Old Testament foretold. Hence John exhibits a positive attitude to the Old Testament but a negative one towards 'the Jews'.

Not only was the author a Jew, he was an eye-witness of the events of the ministry of Jesus. Because of this, he exhibits great freedom in handling the tradition without the fear of losing contact with the historical Jesus. For the other Gospels, the tradition was the only safeguard. Thus the units of the tradition lie close to the surface in those compositions.

The Judaism which forms the background to John was the sectarian Judaism of the Hellenistic age. Jesus' historical confrontation with Judaism is now highlighted in the context of the pressures brought to bear on Jewish Christians. In particular, the Gospel faces the threat of excommunication on the basis of the confession of faith in Jesus. In doing this, John has produced a delicate interweaving of the events of the ministry of Jesus and the implications for the crises of his own day.

Interweaving the situation of Jesus' ministry with that of a later time is linked with the duality of response which is indicated. The limited nature of the response to Jesus and his signs in his own day does not set the limit to the depth of insight which the Gospel may evoke. The use of the misunderstanding motif maintains contact with both situations. Jesus was misunderstood in his own day, and in the context of the Gospel the misunderstandings, as much as the words and works of Jesus, have become the means by which true faith and understanding are evoked.

The misunderstandings which the Gospel explicitly clarifies are those which occur in the context of Judaism. The central point in question is, 'What is Jesus' relation to Moses and the Law?' But the Gospel was written in the Hellenistic age and published in Greek. It was read by non-Jews as well as Jews. The meaning of the Gospel, in the context of Hellenistic paganism as distinct from Hellenistic Judaism, presents us with a different set of problems from those that are explicitly clarified. It is true that the Gospel describes the incarnation of the Word (1.14). But this is not done in the polemical way of 1 John 4. The Gospel does not assert that the divine revealer is really human. Rather it asserts that Jesus of Nazareth is the incarnate Word, the unique Son of the Father. At this point, the Gospel is in conflict with Judaism, not Gnosticism.

The Gospel was produced in a Jewish situation. It partly contributed to a break between Jewish Christians and Judaism. After this break the original Jewish Christian community became open to gentile believers. The new converts understood the Johannine terminology in terms of pagan religious experience rather than the teaching of the Old Testament and salvation history. The new context of understanding produced the crisis which evoked the response of 1 John.

This point of view is stated to indicate that the Johannine language is meaningful against the background of Hellenistic paganism. But understood against that background, the meaning is very different from what it was intended to be, interpreted in the context of Judaism in the Hellenistic age. The recognition of this is vital for a discussion of Johannine symbolism.

There are a number of important Johannine symbols which have a background in both Greek and Hebrew thought. This could suggest that John had deliberately chosen symbols which would have a wide application among people from different backgrounds. The major problem for this view is the fact that the symbols have different meanings according to the background against which they are interpreted. One or two examples should make this point clear.

In the Prologue, Jesus is designated the Logos. Interpreted against a Greek background, this designation could well mean 'Reason', 'Rational', especially if the Greek background presupposed was Stoicism. Many commentators have interpreted Logos in this way. This has often produced a misleading emphasis as well as the omission of a major theme. John's use of Logos occurs in what is generally acknowledged as a theme modelled on Genesis 1. He develops this within a tradition where the creative Word of God has been identified with the Law understood in terms of Wisdom. John's use of Logos is to be understood as Word. God's Word draws attention to God's revealing activity. What is more, Jesus as the Word is not identified with the Law as the Word of God. The Gospel asserts that Jesus, not the Law, is the Word of God. The Law bears witness to him.

Another image affected by background is light. Understood against a Greek religious background, this symbol could be understood in terms of mystical enlightenment. John's use of light has been interpreted in this way. But this overlooks the obvious connection between light as a symbol for the Law in the Old Testament and the context of judgement in which light appears in John. 'This is the judgement, light has come into the world ...' It overlooks the Qumran and Johannine antithesis of light and darkness.

Two characteristics of Johannine symbolism have emerged in this discussion. Firstly, the symbols are christologically oriented. The Johannine symbols replace the Synoptic parables in the framework of the Gospel. A comparison of the relative functions of symbols and parables highlights this christological orientation. Jesus is the Word, the light, the bread of life, the good shepherd, the vine. In the Synoptics, parables sometimes exemplify Jesus' ministry. But there is no explicit identification of Jesus with characters in the parables as there is in the Johannine symbolism.

> This christocentric orientation gives the clue to the interpretation of John 7.37ff. Here, as elsewhere, Jesus is the central figure. In spite of our failure to identify the origin of the quotation, it is clearly out of Jesus' 'belly' that the living waters, the Spirit, flow. While it is grammatically possible that the quotation may refer to the believer and not Jesus, the context in fact excludes this possibility theologically. It is Jesus who calls people to come to him and drink. The quotation comes as an evidence of the reality of what Jesus offers. The evangelist then goes on to indicate the interpretation. The Spirit was not yet given because Jesus was not glorified. But Jesus was about

to give the Spirit to believers. The use of the quotation is christocentric. Jesus is the giver of living water, the Spirit. There can be little doubt that this was in mind also in 19.34; 'Out of his breast came water and blood.'

Secondly, the symbols are always focal points of the conflict between Jesus and Judaism. In the symbol, what Judaism often applied to the Law, or to Israel, is claimed for Jesus, but in a new way. Jesus, not the Law, is the Word of God. But the Word is now understood personally as the unique Son of the Father. Jesus, not Israel, is the vine. But the vine is now distinguished from the branches. Jesus is the Vine and those who believe in him are the branches. He constitutes the possibility. The branches can never be the vine without him.

Once more, in the general examination of symbols, our attention has been turned to John's presentation of the person of Christ. This presentation has presupposed that the significance of the symbols is meaningful only where the confrontation of Jewish Christian with Judaism is already critical.

The question of symbol is also raised by the presentation of the miracles of Jesus as signs. Dodd has interpreted signs in John as symbolic actions, including miracles. He has entitled chapters 2 to 12 as the Book of Signs. He interprets both the cleansing of the temple and the footwashing as signs. On the basis of this interpretation, it is hard to see why the footwashing of chapter 13 is not included in the Book of Signs. There are, in fact, good reasons for noting a division at the end of chapter 12. It ends with a concluding summary of Jesus' public ministry and chapter 13 commences a new phase of Jesus' ministry. This alone is enough to make us question Dodd's view of signs and his title, Book of Signs, especially as 20.30 extends the scope of reference to signs outside the so-called Book of Signs and suggests that Jesus performed other signs (miracles) after his resurrection.

Dodd acknowledges that, in the Gospel, 'sign' always refers to a miracle. But he thinks that the Johannine use is broader. His main evidence for this is the symbolic action of the prophets of the Old Testament. These actions portrayed the coming of the judgement of God (Isa. 20.3; Jer. 13.1–11; Ezek. 12.1–16). But the links with John's use of 'sign' are far from clear. It is true that

John does use the verb, 'to signify', to indicate the manner in which Jesus and Peter would die (12.33; 18.32; 21.19). But the verb need not be used in the same way as the noun. We still have to face the fact that John always uses 'sign' of miracles. What is more, sign is commonly used of miracles in the Synoptics and Acts. While the word is not used in exactly the same way in John, his usage has arisen from the gospel tradition. We find the demand for a sign in John (2.18; 6.30) much as in the Synoptics (Matt. 12.38–39; 16.1–4), and also reference to signs and wonders (John 4.48; Matt. 24.28; Acts 2.23). Of course, the apocalyptic tendency with signs of the end is missing from John.

John's use of 'sign' has its roots in the gospel tradition. But the Old Testament seems to have influenced the development of the theme of signs. In the Exodus event, the people refused to believe, even though God had performed many signs through Moses (Exod. 10.1; Num. 14.11,22; Deut. 7.19), just as the Jews refused to believe in Jesus in spite of the signs he had worked (John 12.37). In both the Old Testament and in John, the description, sign, is indicative of the third-party attitude to miracles achieved. What is more, in both Num. 14.11 and John 12.37, we are told of the failure of the signs to lead to faith. But, of course, the Gospel indicates that after the resurrection the witness of the signs effectively leads to authentic faith.

We have observed that the characteristic description of the miracles by Jesus is 'works'. Only in 4.48 and 6.26 does Jesus speak of signs, and there he is speaking of the viewpoint of those who had seen his works. Of course Jesus can refer to his whole ministry as his work (17.4). But characteristically Jesus refers to the miracles as works. This use also has a precedent in the Synoptics (Matt. 11.2; Luke 24.19). But it has become characteristic in John. Again the Old Testament influence seems to be evident. There creation is the work of God (Genesis 2.2), as are also the miraculous saving acts of the Exodus (Exod. 34.10, etc.). In John, Jesus' miracles are the creative and saving works of God.

Jesus' works, or signs, draw our attention to the one whose signs and works are reminiscent of Moses. But a greater than Moses is here. Of course, John was not content that Jesus' works should be viewed as bare miracles, marvels. He was not satisfied with the view of Jesus as a mere miracle-worker. Thus the miracles do not remain uninterpreted. The miracles, signs, become the basis of extended discourses. But not every discourse has its roots in a miracle, not every discourse has a sign to elaborate. The good shepherd is a symbolic discourse, but not a sign. The signs are always miracles which, for John, have become the vehicle for communicating the challenge of Jesus' person and work.

Here we have what is unique about the signs in John. He has selected seven miracles from a great fund of material in order that the implications concerning Jesus may become clear. Only the miracle at the wedding at Cana is unique to John. But the six miracles which he has in common with the Synoptics serve a different purpose in John. Here they are the subject for the development of discourse. The discourses are christocentric. They derive their symbolism from the signs (miracles). But the signs are not simply symbolic stories. The symbolic discourses elucidate the meaning of the miracles for our understanding of the person and work of Jesus.

Whereas the miracles are signs of the inbreaking of the kingdom of God in the Synoptics (an expression used only twice in John 3.3,5), in John the signs reveal the true significance of Jesus to those who believe (20.30–31).

Of course the symbolic discourses which are not rooted in signs also reveal the true significance of Jesus for faith. But the fact that many of the discourses are rooted in signs, indicates that the truth which is presented in the discourses is not that of abstract ideals, but actual truth expressed in events. The God who is revealed here is not known in the mystical flight from history but in his actions in the world of history.

The inseparable connection between discourses and signs indicates that we are not dealing with bare events, but events with direction, meaning and purpose. God has not only achieved certain events. He has declared their direction, value, meaning and purpose, in his Son, whom we therefore call the Word of God. The theme of revelation is also christocentric.

2 *The Revelation of the Word*

The theme of revelation, God's revealing activity, is expressed at the beginning of the Gospel, where Jesus is designated the Logos, the Word of God. C. H. Dodd has given an impressive list of parallels between the Prologue of John and the Wisdom literature (*The Interpretation of the Fourth Gospel*, p. 274f.). Of course, useful additions could be made to this list, but they would only confirm the conclusions already clear from the comparisons given. Especially important are references in the Qumran texts where the function of creation is attributed to God's knowledge, Wisdom and the Law. John's use of Logos is dependent on a tradition where the Word of God, the Law and Wisdom had become identified. The themes of pre-existence, creation and revelation were already united in this tradition which also spoke of Wisdom, the Law, coming to tabernacle amongst men, making them friends of God, a theme developed in John 1.14. Thus the theme of revelation is set in the context of the question of the relationship of Judaism and Christianity.

John does not make much use of the technical terminology of revelation, but the theme is central to the Gospel and is given expression in the Logos of the opening verses. The fact that the Logos designation is used only in the Prologue has led to speculation as to whether a source hymn might have provided John with this material. The 'poetic' style of this section, which is similar to Wisdom poetry, is thought by some to confirm this view. But, as Bultmann has noted, this poetic style is not confined to the Prologue. It is to be found also in the Johannine discourses. This has led Bultmann to suggest a common source behind the Prologue and the discourses which he has called 'the Revelation discourses'. Alternatively, C. K. Barrett suggests that the Prologue was a specially written introduction to the Gospel, introducing the major themes to be developed in the Gospel. In view of the convincing evidence of the basic unity of the Gospel, this view seems to be sound. Even if John used a source hymn (and we do not know that he did), he regarded the Prologue in its present form as a valid introduction to his Gospel.

The Wisdom parallels point away from Gnosticism to a treatment of the theme of the Law in relation to the Christian revelation. In this exposition, John has used words, ideas and forms from the Wisdom literature.

But John designates Jesus as Logos, not Law or Wisdom. Of course Word, Law and Wisdom had come to be used interchangeably in the Wisdom tradition. John chose Logos. Law was excluded because John wished to contrast the incarnate Logos with the Law. This contrast was a major reason for John's development of the theme of revelation and use of the Logos designation.

Wisdom was unsuitable because it is a feminine noun. More important is the fact that there was an undesirable Wisdom tradition. Paul encountered this (twenty-three of the twenty-eight uses of 'Wisdom' in the New Testament occur in the letters of Paul and all but two of these are in 1 Corinthians, Ephesians and Colossians, where Paul confronted Wisdom, falsely so-called), asserting that Christ is the true Wisdom from God.

John chose Logos because it expressed the theme of revelation dynamically, drawing a number of themes together.

1. John 1.1 recalls Genesis 1.1 understood as creation by the Word of God as in Psalm 33.6. Thus the incarnate Word is understood as the creative Word of God and the created order is understood as a reality created, not just by an act of power but by the Word.

2. With the Old Testament in mind, the significance of the Prophetic Word cannot be overlooked. The creative Word and the Prophetic Word are one in Jesus (1.6ff., 15ff.; 5.39,46; 8.56,58; 12.41). The themes of creation and revelation are prominently united in the Prologue and this relation is basic for the Gospel.

3. Jesus, who is the Word of God, speaks God's words (17.8,14). He communicates himself in his words. To receive his words is to receive him, to abide in his words is to abide in him (6.35ff.; 15.1ff.; 17.1ff.).

4. John wanted to draw attention to the fact that the Word

proclaimed by the Church was Jesus, a theme which has links with Paul's thought (in Romans 1.16–17; 1 Corinthians 1.18–30) but goes beyond Paul in designating Jesus as the Word.

THE FATHER—
THE ORIGIN OF THE REVELATION

The statement that God (the Father) always has his Word is an indication of the nature, or character of God. Words indicate disclosure. Words are the basic means of communication. The Word is not withheld in silence. It is uttered. God is the God who reveals himself, for the Word is eternal, with God, the Word of God. The Word revealed is a self-communication, for God himself is the subject of the revelation. His will to reveal himself arises from his character; it is his will for the coming of his kingdom, his will for fellowship (1 John 1.3).

Ultimately, the question of why God reveals himself can only be answered, because he is the God who reveals himself. But this may be expressed in a little more detail. Revelation occurs because of God's love for the world (3.16). God's love is the reason for the existence of the created order, the world. The nature of that love is revealed as self-giving love in the giving of the Son. Thus the incarnation of the Word arose out of and expresses the Father's love for the world (1.17; 1 John 4.9–10). But no answer can be given to the question of why God loves the world except to say 'God is love' (1 John 4.8).

The coming of the revelation is described in terms of the Son's mission from the Father. This indicates that the Father is the source of the revelation. Jesus' mission is described by him in terms of his coming, of his being sent, but the most characteristic description is of 'The Father who sent me', which is used 24 times (4.34; 5.23,24,30,37; 6.38,39,44; 7.16(18),28,33; 8.16,18,26,29; 9.4; 12.44,45,49; 13.20; 14.24; 15.21; 16.5). Reference to Jesus' mission in these terms has its roots in the Synoptic tradition. Parallels with the sayings in John occur there. But this usage has been developed systematically into a major feature in John.

The description of Jesus' mission in these terms revealed that his authority was grounded in the Father who participates in his activity (5.36; 6.57). This is done in such a way that attention is drawn to Jesus as the prophet like Moses of Deut. 18.15,18–19 and also referred to in the Qumran texts (1 QS 9.11; 4 Q Test.). John is not the only writer in the New Testament to make this identification (Acts 3.22–23; 7.37). Here again we find the contrast between Jesus and Moses in the Gospel.

Jesus as the Prophet demonstrated his status by the performance of prophetic signs. The signs revealed that he had come from God, at least in the prophetic sense. Thus many people recognize him as a prophet (3.2; 4.19; 9.16–17) or *the* prophet (6.14), the Messianic prophet (7.26,40f.). Just as the prophets of old claimed to stand in the council of the Lord to hear his Word, so Jesus claimed such a relation for himself (1.18; 5.19–20, etc.).

While John highlights the recognition of Jesus as the prophet, this is only the starting-point for his Christology. Those who recognize Jesus in this way are challenged to see the revelation of God in Jesus, as the one who is more than a prophet (4.41–42; 5.24ff.; 6.34–35,48,50–51; 8.58; 9.35–38). The prophetic model has been used because Jesus was so acknowledged in his own day, and it provided a means of showing that Jesus' authority and mission came from the Father. The descent of the Spirit on Jesus is described, emphasizing the permanent abiding of the Spirit upon him (1.32; 3.34). But Jesus is not a Spirit-endowed man. He is the one who bestows the Spirit (1.33; 7.38–39; 15.26; 16.7), as Moses desired, but himself was unable to do (Numb. 11.29). Again in this way, John shows, a greater than Moses is here.

Jesus' mission, one could say his apostleship, emphasizes that he has come from the Father to do the Father's will. He did not come as an inspired man. He came as the incarnate Word. His dignity and greatness were not expressed in independence but in total dependence on the Father. Jesus as the one sent, as the Word of the Father, is the full expression of the Father because of his total dependence upon him. It was his life to do the Father's will.

Jesus also claims that he is himself the central fact of the revelation. Because of this, Jesus' self-revelation will be a major aspect of our study of revelation.

Our focus on the theme of revelation has necessarily been a focus on Christology. John presents us with a Logos Christology, and the emphasis on mission and dependence shows that we are to understand Jesus as the Word of the Father. To know him is to know the Father. The same point is made by describing Jesus as the unique Son of the Father who makes the Father known (1.18). His Sonship indicates his dependence on the Father and his ability to make the Father known. That this revealing activity is his characteristic work is made clear by describing Jesus as the Word, Logos.

Before passing to the next aspect of the theme, it will be useful to note that Bultmann rejects the christological aspect of the statements about revelation. He argues that John was using a Gnostic myth to indicate the nature of the revelation. Thus the statements about the eternity of the Word and his coming into the world are not statements relating to a person, the Word, the Son. The statements refer to the revelation. They indicate that God's revelation has occurred in this man, Jesus of Nazareth. The revelation has come, it does not belong to this world, it is eternal. But Jesus of Nazareth is not eternal, has not come from heaven into the world. The statements to this effect indicate only his significance to us as the Revealer.

Two criticisms can be made briefly. Firstly, evidence for the existence of the myth to which Bultmann refers, prior to the writing of the Gospel, is completely lacking. Secondly, John gives no indication that he is using myth in the way Bultmann suggests. The obvious meaning concerns the person of the Son, the Word, who was incarnate in Jesus of Nazareth. John affirms that Jesus is the revealer because of his relation to the Father as the Word, the Son of the Father. Thus Jesus reveals the Father to us because he is himself the eternal Word, the Son of the Father, who has come from the Father into the world.

We may turn now to discuss the revealing work of the Word.

CREATION BY THE WORD— GENERAL REVELATION

The theme of revelation is introduced in such a way that the nature of God as the revealer is indicated. His will to reveal himself underlies the whole of existence. This is his will for the coming of his kingdom. It does not arise out of a personal need but from self-giving love (3.16). The revelation event is rooted in being, God's being. The love event has its origin in God's being (1 John 4.8).

By speaking of creation by the Word, John gives expression to some idea of general revelation. God was revealing himself in creative activity. But the world rejected that revelation (1.10). What kind of revelation is it that is not received by those for whom it was intended? It is a revelation which makes blameworthy man's failure to know God in his creative work. Man who rejects this revelation is not left as he was (9.39ff.; cf. Romans 1.18ff.).

What is the nature of this revelation? Bultmann suggests that man should have understood himself as God's creature and every man is, or once was, faced with the decision for or against this possibility. Knowledge of creatureliness is not grounded in any emotion or feeling, but in existential self-knowledge. The world is originally intelligible as creation. So also is God's claim on man as his creature, the claim that man should honour God (cf. Rom. 1.18–21).

In general terms, this line of interpretation is helpful. Looked at in detail, certain criticisms would need to be made. Existential self-knowledge is linked with the interpretation of 1.4. Bultmann interprets this as meaning that the life created by the Word was light for men. The light is the authentic self-understanding of true life. But 'the light for men' is the light of the Word. All men come under the judgement of the light (3.19). They always have come under the judgement of the light, whether they have known it or not. The existence of the darkness does not overcome the light. The rejection of the light is not a denial of judgement, but a manifestation of it. Not all men have rejected the light, and we will turn in a moment to the witness of those who received the light.

Generally speaking, John's thought is clear. The world stands condemned because of its rejection of the knowledge of God, whether understood in terms of Romans 1.18ff., or in terms of 'natural law', as in Romans 2.14–15; 5.12–14. There is no clarity at this point. But, in some way, the unfulfilled possibility for the world stands in judgement over the world as it is now. The lack of clarity is not surprising, as we are dealing only with a background aspect of the theme of revelation in John.

Before turning to the witness to the revelation, something needs to be said about the treatment of the world (*kosmos*) in John. The word is used 78 times in the Gospel, 23 times in 1 John, but only 15 times in the Synoptics. In the New Testament, only in 1 Corinthians, where the word is used 21 times, does any book come near to this concentration of interest in the world, and 1 Corinthians 1.21 should be compared with John 1.10.

John speaks of the world sometimes as God's creation, but more frequently in terms of the lost possibility. Darkness is of the essence of the world as it now is (8.12; 12.35,46). The revelation comes as the light of judgement, causing division, bringing condemnation and life.

The world is the world of men who love the darkness rather than the light (3.19); who are blind but claim to have sight (9.39–41); who are in bondage to sin but claim to be free (8.34); and as a consequence are under the sway of death (8.21,24). The world, which claims to have knowledge, freedom and life, has only a lie, the darkness. It does not know God, nor does it recognize the revealer or the Spirit. But this is the world God loved, and in this world the Word became flesh. Creation by the Word is the presupposition necessary for revelation. The grace of revelation is given, but only those who have integrity, who do the truth, come to the light.

Already John has made extremely important statements for the readers of his day and ours. Creation and redemption are bound together despite the fact that the world, as it is now, does not know God. God's revelation and the possibility of man's response can only be understood on the basis of the recognition that the world was created by the Word. How the world came to be as it now is is not explained, though we will notice certain hints at a later stage. That the world may fulfil its lost possibility is due to the fact that it was created by the Word and the Father's love for it has not ceased, in spite of the fact that it has rejected the knowledge of God. Of course, not all men belong to the world in that sense, though it is true that they once did so belong, even the disciples (17.6). Those who have received the revelation no longer belong to the world but bear witness to the light.

THE REVELATION OF THE WORD IN THE LAW AND THE PROPHETS

Revelation was not confined to creation. For this possibility of knowing God remained unfulfilled. John affirms that the Word, through whom creation has its being, was revealed to Moses and the prophets. Because of this, Moses and the prophets bear witness to Jesus (5.39,45–47; 12.41). Even Abraham rejoiced to see Jesus' day (8.56).

John makes clear that the function of the Law and the Prophets is witness to Jesus, the Word made flesh. This theme finds repeated emphasis with John the Baptist, who represents the prophetic tradition. John interprets the Baptist's role wholly in terms of his witness to Jesus (1.6–8,15,19ff.; 3.22, etc.).

Possession of the Old Testament should have led the Jews to believe in Jesus. Thus their failure to do so is the more reprehensible (1.11), because the Old Testament gave them the knowledge of God and of the way to worship him (4.21–24). But this revelation moved towards and bore witness to the saving act of God in Christ. His coming brought an end to all religious quests and transformed the role of the Old Testament so that it has become a witness to the new revelation event.

The one Word is revealed in the witness of the Old Testament and the Word made flesh. There is a continuity of salvation history. But the coming of the Word made flesh has fulfilled the witness of the Old Testament and abolished its significance as a closed system. Thus John affirms that the Old Testament reveals God only when it is read as a book which witnesses to the Word who became flesh in Jesus of Nazareth.

Bultmann's rejection of the salvation history perspective in John does violence to this basic theme, the relation of Jesus to the Old Testament. This perspective is crucial for John's understanding of revelation. Jesus does not come without a long history of preparation. The history of Israel is fundamental for John's understanding of the preparation for the coming of the

Word made flesh. Salvation history is a focal point of history where God's saving action is to be seen, coming to fulfilment in Jesus.

By drawing attention to the witness of the Old Testament, John shows that the Jews should have believed in Jesus and are condemned by the Scriptures in which they put their trust (5.45).

THE REVELATION OF THE WORD MADE FLESH AS THE LIGHT OF THE WORLD

The coming of revelation in Jesus, the Word made flesh (1.14ff.), was to save the world (3.17; 12.47). But this coming involved judgement (3.19; 9.39ff.), because of the nature of the world. This revelation is designed for the sinful world which is in darkness. The Word made flesh is the light for the world (1.4,9; 8.12; 9.5; cf. 3.19–21; 12.46).

> The light symbolism, like the other symbols used in John, has its background in Judaism and in the gospel tradition and has a christocentric focus; Matt. 4.16 cites Isa. 9.1; Luke 2.32 cites Isa. 42.6; 49.6. In Matt. 5.14, the disciples are described as 'the light of the world' as Jesus is in John 8.12, etc. (cf. Ps. 27.1). By going a stage behind the Synoptic saying, John indicates that the Church's witness is grounded in the work of Jesus. He, not the Law (Psalm 119.105), is the light for men.

The revelation event is described as the coming of 'the true light' to which the Baptist (1.8) and the Scriptures (5.39) bore witness. They are lights (5.35), but not the true light. 'True' here is not opposed to 'false', but makes clear the secondary nature of the witness of the Baptist and the Old Testament and the primary significance of Jesus. There were witnesses to the light before the coming of Jesus into the world, but at his coming they were rendered obsolete (1.9; 3.19 (8.12; 9.5) 12.46).

Three things are clear about the revelation as the light—the judgement of the world, and are emphasized in chapters 8 and 9.

(*a*) The revelation causes division.
(*b*) The revelation is the condemnation of the false life and religion of the world.
(*c*) The revelation is the opportunity to come to authentic life.

The judgement of the light causes division (3.19; 12.31)

Jesus' coming into the world was for the purpose of judgement (9.39ff.). This appears to contradict 3.17. Different Greek words are used in the two verses, but it is the contexts which indicate the distinction of meaning. In 3.17, the judgement is condemnation, as the contrast with salvation shows, but in 9.39 the idea includes both condemnation and salvation. Thus Jesus did not come with the purpose of condemning. He came to cause division in order that men might be saved. But some men would also be condemned. By worldly standards, this division is no judgement at all.

> All of the references to the light occur in chapters 1—12, which deal with the revelation to the world, the challenge of the light to the darkness (3.19–21). A recurring theme in this section is the divisions which Jesus caused (7.43; 9.16; 10.19), as men leave the darkness for the light (9.5,25,39,41). During chapters 1—12, the light shines in the darkness. The Jews deny Jesus' claims (10.1–41), deny the meaning of his miracles (11.1–54), deny the witness of those who believe (11.55—12.9), and thus retreat irrevocably into the darkness of falsehood and death. All of this suggests that chapters 1—12 could appropriately be called, 'The light shines in the darkness'. In chapters 13—17, Jesus is present with those who believe in him. Division has already taken place, and only Judas has to divide himself off from the community of believers. John adds significantly, 'and it was night' (13.30). Judas withdraws into the darkness and his condemnation is sealed.

The judgement of the light is the condemnation of the world

The life revealed in Jesus condemns what the world calls life (1.4). Once again the theme is expressed in conflict with the views of Judaism. It is the Jews who claim to have life. The claim is expressed symbolically in the claim to have sight (9.39–41). Because they thought they had life, they rejected the possibility of life which had come in Jesus. By rejecting the revelation, they are condemned definitively and irrevocably to the darkness because, having rejected the light, there is no possible cure for their blindness.

The Jews thought that they had life. What they sought to do was safeguard and preserve the life which they had. Their basic error was in thinking that they knew the way of life and already possessed it. It was thought that water and bread would sustain life (4.15; 6.26). Thus these elements are sought.

Of course, in chapter 6, the fact that bread is a symbol for Law is also in mind. Thus we have the contrast between Moses, the giver of manna and the Law, and Jesus, the giver of the true bread from heaven. In that discourse, bread becomes the symbol for Jesus' life-giving activity in giving himself for the life of the world. In this way Jesus shows that true life does not come from bread or water. But his use of these symbols suggests that there is a connection between the life for which the world longs, distorted though that longing may be, and the life revealed in him. Because the Jews took the symbol for the reality, they failed to understand their need of life, they failed to see that Jesus had brought them the possibility of having true life. Thus Jesus not only condemned their quest for life, he condemned their understanding of religion.

The Jews claimed that they had life by virtue of their possession of the Scriptures (5.39). But it was this claim which prevented them from coming to Jesus (5.40). Ironically, they did not understand that it was to Jesus, as the Lord and giver of life, that the Scriptures bore witness. By their interpretation of the Old Testament in legal terms, as a book providing precedents, they limited God's action to what he had done in the past. They could accept a repetition, but not something new which went beyond the limits of what the Old Testament had already recorded. But, in John, Jesus insists that the Old Testament is a book which points beyond itself in its witness to the action of the eternal Word in creation and revelation. In particular, its witness is to be understood in terms of the movement of salvation history which came to its fulfilment when the eternal Word became flesh and dwelt among us. By their interpretation, which rejected the witness of the Old Testament to the movement from the lesser revelation to the greater, the Jews perverted the word of God so that it became, for them, the mere word of man, or even worse, the word of the devil (8.38–47).

The condemnation of the Jew's quest for religion is emphasized in 2.13–22; 4.1–42; 5.1–47 and in chapters 7—9. It becomes quite clear that the rejection of life is not properly understood until it is seen to be, at the same time, the rejection of God. Thus it is a genuine religious question. For the Jews used their religion to safeguard themselves from the revelation (5.18; 6.42; 7.22–24,27, 48–52; 9.16,24). This is a recurring theme in chapters 5—9. Religion which makes men secure against the revelation is condemned by Jesus.

The quests for life and religion prove to be a common quest. The revelation in Jesus condemns both, for the life revealed in him is also the truth (14.6), not truth in general, but the truth which God is, which is his Word (17.17). The truth is the revelation of God in Jesus, who speaks the truth, does the truth, and is the truth, who in his whole being, words and works, is the revelation of God.

The coming of the revelation in Jesus was the fulfilment of the hope to which the Old Testament bore witness. But it condemned the religious quest of Judaism along with that of all other religions (4.22–24). The witness of the Old Testament should have led the Jews to believe in Jesus. Their failure to receive that witness brought their religion, with the religions of the world, of which it had now become one, under the condemnation of the revelation. Because Jesus' coming was expressly to save (not condemn), not all Jews rejected Jesus but condemnation was the consequence of rejection.

The Word made flesh as the life-giving light

For those who admit that they need life, are blind, in the darkness, the coming of the light is the opportunity to have life, to see, to be in the light, to become children of the light (3.19–21; 8.12; 9.39; 12.35–36, 46). Jesus is the light, the revelation, for the world of sinful men (1.4; 8.12; 9.5). His revelation judges the world. He is also the light, revelation, of life (1.4; 8.12). In him the true nature of life has been revealed (cf. 1 John 1.2), and for those who receive him there is the gift of life. For the light of life is also the life-giving light, life-giving to all who follow (8.12)

The judgement brought about by the coming of the light is seen as a dividing of men according to their response to the revelation. Those who reject are condemned, and those who accept the revelation receive the gift of life (3.19–21,36; 9.16,39–41). John's use of the symbol of light is christocentric, and highlights the conflict with Judaism. Light concentrates attention on the judgement brought about by the revelation. In doing this, John portrays Jesus' self-revelation, because what stands in judgement over the world is the truth, which Jesus claims to be.

3 Jesus' Self-revelation

Jesus' most startling claim was that he himself is the revelation of God. In revealing himself he revealed God. We have already seen how this revelation stood over against the ideas of God, religion and life in Judaism. We need now to see how all the claims centre on Jesus himself. While there are those who bear witness to him, ultimately it is his own claims about himself which cannot be ignored. These claims are characteristically set out in statements that are recognized by the use of the formula, 'I am ...'.

Many readers of the Gospel are put off by these statements. The form of them suggests that Jesus is preoccupied with his own importance. But to come to this conclusion is only possible if we ignore what it is that Jesus claims to be. Thus the contexts of the statements are all important.

Twenty-six of the thirty uses of 'I am' in John occur on the lips of Jesus. In the four other instances, no mysterious sense is attached, and in ten of the statements by Jesus the object of the 'I am' is clearly stated or implied. Thus Jesus claims to be Jesus of Nazareth, the Messiah, the Son of Man. From this it can be seen that no special theological meaning should be read into the use of the 'I am ...' formula in itself.

But there are a number of instances where 'I am' is used without a supplied or implied object. This may be called the absolute use of 'I am', and it is unintelligible Greek. In the Greek version of the Old Testament, 'I am' is used absolutely by God, and sometimes by the arrogant sinner who puts himself in the place of God (Isa. 47.8; Zeph. 2.15). The 'I am' is used of God where his eternal being is stressed. Of course, the complete form is 'I am God' (Isa. 43.13; 46.4; 48.12; 52.6; Deut. 32.39). The eternal God, who controls history, stands over against the powerless pretensions of deity worshipped by the heathen.

> The suggestion that the absolute use of 'I am' is a play on the divine name of Exod. 3.14–16 is just possible. But Bultmann has shown that reference to this really requires the repetition of 'I am'. If this objection is set aside, this suggestion adds weight to what John says about believing in the name of Jesus (1.12).

In John, the absolute use of 'I am' occurs where Jesus asserts his eternal being over against all false claims. The false claims in view are not those of the heathen religions, but those of Judaism (8.24,28,58; 13.19). In Jesus, the Word made flesh, the eternal 'I am' is encountered.

Not all of the theologically important uses of 'I am' occur in the absolute form. There are thirteen statements where Jesus uses 'I am' with a symbolic object, and these may be arranged in seven different groups where Jesus claims:

1. I am the bread of life (6.35,41,48).
2. I am the light of the world (8.12; 9.5).
3. I am the door (10.7,9).
4. I am the good shepherd (10.11,14).
5. I am the resurrection and the life (11.25).
6. I am the way, the truth and the life (14.6).
7. I am the true vine (15.1,5).

> It is interesting to notice that John describes in detail 7 miraculous signs and reports 7 symbolic 'I am' statements. But not all of the statements occur in the so-called 'Book of Signs', and the majority are not made in the context of a miraculous sign. It is difficult to know whether or not the number 7 has an attraction for John. It could be pure coincidence that we have these 2 groups of 7.

Bultmann describes five of these symbolic statements (all but 5 and 6) as 'Recognition formulae', in which the symbol is the subject and the 'I' is the object (as in Isa. 41.4; 43.10f.; 52.6; Deut. 32.39). Jesus announces that he is the one for whom the people are searching. But a new interpretation is given so that the 'I am' stands in contrast to the false expectation. We have seen this already in terms of light as the condemnation of the quest for religion and life.

While there is something positive in this approach, it overlooks the fact that the absolute form asserts the eternal being of the Word incarnate, not simply the eternity of the revelation. The stress is on the person, who he is, as well as what his significance is for men. Nor is it fair to say, as Bultmann does, that the various symbols make the same point. Naturally, they have something in common, because they are the object of Jesus' 'I am' statement.

Bultmann claims that the symbols 'bread of life' and 'living water' have the same meaning. But he has failed to note that Jesus gives the 'living water', which is not the object of an 'I am' statement as is 'bread of life'. 'Water' is interpreted as the Spirit (4.10; 7.38–39). Jesus and the Spirit are closely related, but not identified (4.23,24) and the meaning of the symbol 'light', indicating judgement, has already been noted.

Bultmann describes 11.25 and 14.6 as Identification formulae in which the 'I' is the subject and the object defines the character or identity of the subject. The stress is not wholly on the 'I' because Jesus describes what he is for man, and the meaning of his mission in terms of the symbolic object. Different aspects of Jesus' mission are portrayed in the seven statements suggesting that the other five (Recognition formulae) should not be understood as being completely different from the Identification formulae.

What is positive about Bultmann's approach is that it notes the way the 'I am' statements are given form by the false expectations. But what the symbols indicate is that Jesus' new revelation is set over against Judaism and the Law. This becomes clear from a brief examination of these 7 'I am ...' statements.

Jesus is the bread of life, 6.35(41),48

Bread was used as a symbol for the Law, thought of as a life-giving principle (Sirach 15.3; 24.19–21; cf. John 5.39). Jesus asserts that he, not the Law, gives life. Moses gave the people bread (manna) and the Law. Jesus gave the multitude bread and claims that the Father, not Moses, gives the true bread from heaven. That bread is Jesus himself (6.32–33,35,41,48,50–51). It is also said that Jesus gives the bread, but as he does only the Father's will this is not a contradiction. Jesus (and the Father), not Moses, gives the true life-giving bread. Jesus, not the Law, is that bread. Jesus is the bread of life. Only because of who he is, is he able to give the life-giving bread. The giving of the bread became a reality when Jesus gave his flesh over to death in order that the world might have life.

> John does not present a sacramental view at this point. John 6.51ff. appears to combat a Jewish misunderstanding about the observance of 'the last supper'. Jesus is the reality symbolized by bread. Eating the bread is understood symbolically to indicate coming to him and believing in him as the one who brings life (6.35,63). The discussion of the new birth (3.3–8) is to be understood in the same way. New birth (regeneration) comes about through believing in Jesus, through receiving him (3.16 and 1.12). In the Johannine situation public baptism was a challenge to those who wished to be secret believers. John is not a sacramentalist unless we mean by this that he presents Jesus and the reality that he brings under the cover of evocative symbols.

Jesus is the light of the world (8.12; 9.5; see p. 33ff. above)

Light was also a symbol for the Law (Psalm 119.105). Thus Jesus claims that he, not the Law, has brought about the judgement of the world. Judgement is the primary function of the revelation portrayed as light. But Psalm 27 teaches, 'The Lord is my light and my salvation ...'. In John, it is clear that the judgement brought about by Jesus has a positive side for those who believe they have life from the light of the world. Because Jesus is the light of the world, he came into the world and the world was judged by his coming (3.19–21; 9.39–41; 15.22–24).

Jesus is the door (10.7,9), the way (14.6)

These symbols assert the exclusive nature of Jesus' being and activity as the revelation of God. While 'the door' in 10.1–6 i the means by which the shepherd enters, in 10.7ff. Jesus is the only door by which the sheep enter life. The parable of 10.1–6 appears to have been taken up again in 10.11ff. That parable shares with 10.7ff. the assertion of Jesus' exclusive role. In 10.7ff. he alone is the one through whom men find life. All others who have claimed this role for themselves, the Messianic pretenders and the false saviours, are thieves and robbers. It is likely that the interpretation of the role of Moses in Judaism is also confronted by this statement.

> The contrast with Moses and the Law is suggested by the Symbol 'the way' which is frequently used in the Old Testament as a symbol for the Law (Deut. 1.30ff.; 5.32f.; 31.15–19; 31.29 and in numerous Psalms). It is also used this way in the Qumran texts. 'The way' is a symbol also found in the gospel tradition (Mark 9.43,45,47; Matthew 7.7,13f.; 18.8f.).

Jesus is 'the door' to life because he is 'the way' to the Father (14.6). In 14.4–5, 'the way' Jesus must take to return to the Father is in view, that is, his death on the cross. Only in 14.6 is it said that Jesus is 'the way' men must take to come to the Father. Thus, like 'the door', 'the way' is a symbol which describes both the activity of Jesus and the disciples. 'The door' is the means by which the shepherd comes to the sheep: 'the way' refers to the means by which he returns to the Father. For the disciples, Jesus is both 'the door' to life and 'the way' to the Father.

Bultmann has a fine section in his commentary which deals with the exclusiveness of the revelation. This is certainly the point of 10.7,9; 14.6. But we need to go beyond Bultmann and recognize that John asserts that there is exclusively one door, one way, because Jesus is 'the door', 'the way'. In other words, John's view of revelation is rooted in his view of Christ. Because he is the unique Son of the Father in a unique relation to the Father, he and he alone can make him known (1.18). Thus Jesus is the Word of the Father. He speaks only what he has heard from the Father (8.26) and his whole life is the fulfilment of the Father's will (5.30; 4.34). He does only what he sees the Father doing, and because the Father shows him all that he does, this means that he does all that the Father does (5.19–20). He is the complete, perfect revelation of the Father. To receive Jesus is to receive the Father.

Jesus, 'the way', is not as other ways, to be discarded once the goal is reached. He is also the truth, the way and the truth together because the truth can only be known by coming again and again by the way. God is known only by believing in Jesus, coming to Jesus (6.35,37) and those who believe are challenged to abide in his words, to continue in faith. To those who abide in faith, Jesus promised the knowledge of the truth (8.31–32).

Because Jesus is the way, all generations of Christians stand in the same relation to the revelation. None can dispense with the way, not even the apostles. There is no outgrowing the revelation event. Of course, the apostles stood in a direct relation to Jesus, but, as we shall see, the revelation only became effective, even for them, after Jesus had returned to the Father and the Paraclete, the Spirit of truth, had come.

Jesus is the good shepherd (10.11,14)

The good shepherd is contrasted with thieves and robbers (10.10) and the hireling (10.12).

> In the Old Testament, the shepherd symbol is used of God and the leaders of the nation (Ps. 23; 78.70–72; 80; Isa. 40.11; Jer. 31.10; Ezek. 34; 37.24). At Qumran, the Teacher of Righteousness was called 'a faithful shepherd', which approaches the meaning of 'good shepherd' in John, but lacks the exclusivism of '*the* good shepherd'. The symbol of the shepherd is also rooted in the gospel tradition (Mark 6.34; 14.27; Matt. 9.36; 18.12–24; 25.32; 26.31; Luke 15.3–7).

The thieves and robbers are the false shepherds, the leaders of Israel, as in Ezekiel 34. The people refused to hear them because their behaviour indicated that they were not true shepherds. They sought personal gain, but the good shepherd would seek life for the sheep, even at the cost of his own life (10.10,11).

By definition, Jesus alone qualifies as the good shepherd, because the sheep belong to him (10.12,14,27). Not even Peter qualifies as a shepherd, he is an 'hireling' (10.12) and it is Jesus' sheep that he is to tend and feed (21.15–17). Jesus as the good shepherd asserted his rightful ownership of the sheep. In the Gospel, this claim rests on the fact that the world was made by him.

> In the Gospels, the word 'good' (in the phrase 'the good shepherd') is frequently used of fruit, works, trees, ground, seed, pearls, fish, circumstances, salt and measure. In John, it is used only of wine (2.10), the shepherd (10.11,14) and works (10.32–33). 'Good', in this sense, indicates the proper fulfilment of a function. Thus Jesus is the shepherd who behaves as shepherds should, a marked contrast with the false shepherds of Israel. As such, attention is drawn to God as the true shepherd of Israel.

The function of the good shepherd is portrayed in terms of his concern for the sheep to the extent of giving his life for them. The wording of 10.11, like that of 6.51, shows that Jesus' death was no accident, nor was it the result of a moment of enthusiasm. His death was a consequence of his being the good shepherd and this turns us back again to his relation to the Father (10.14–15).

Jesus is the resurrection and the life (11.25f.; 14.6)

The raising of Lazarus introduces the question of eschatology. What view of the last things does John expound? When informed of the death of Lazarus, Jesus affirmed that he would rise again (11.23), which Martha understood in terms of the last day (11.24). This was natural enough because resurrection was thought of as an event of the last day. Jesus did not deny that this would be the case with Lazarus. In addition he drew attention to his own present significance (11.25). Thus the Lazarus event is to be understood as a sign with two levels of meaning.

1. The believer 'who lives' shall never die (11.26) having already passed from death to life (5.24). But this does not exclude physical death, for even Jesus, who is 'the life', gave 'himself' up to death. Nevertheless, eternal life is experienced in the present, pointing to Jesus' present significance. The raising of Lazarus also pointed to Jesus' present significance—and beyond.

2. Lazarus, raised to life, was to die physically again, as many believers had died. But this resurrection pointed beyond itself to the resurrection on the last day (6.40). The eternal life, experienced now, cannot be terminated, not even by death. The believer

will live for ever (6.51,58; 8.51–52; 10.28; 11.26). The gift of life in the present will only be revealed fully at the resurrection on the last day.

'Resurrection' terminology betrays Jewish antecedents, as does 'eternal life', which is derived from the Jewish doctrine of the two ages. The question concerning eternal life is also raised in the Synoptics (Mark 10.17). But the primary emphasis there concerns the kingdom of God, a phrase used only in John 3.3,5. John uses the themes of eternal life and Son of Man in preference to the kingdom of God. He preferred eternal life because:

(*a*) He wished to break with the nationalistic misunderstanding bound up with kingdom of God terminology (1.49; 6.15; 12.12ff.; 18.36).
(*b*) He wished to present Jesus, not the Law (Wisdom), as the one who gives life (Proverbs 8.35).
(*c*) He emphasizes the present personal experience of salvation. Kingdom terminology is corporate and expresses the unfulfilled situation.
(*d*) He wrote during the King's absence, who now reigned through the witness of the Spirit in the Church.

Thus John developed the idea of eternal life, which was in the gospel tradition, to indicate the salvation given to those who believe in Jesus (3.15,16,36; 10.28; 17.2; 20.30f.). Paul also uses this terminology (Romans 6.23).

The present experience of salvation is spoken of in terms of eternal life while resurrection looks to the fulfilment of that experience in the future. But John speaks of 'life' as well as 'eternal life'. 'Life' and 'eternal life' may be used interchangeably. But 'eternal life' is never used of the Father or the Son, they have 'life' in themselves (1.4; 5.26). God is not a transitory being. Therefore the qualification 'eternal' is not needed. Nor does this mean simply that the Father and Son are alive. They have the power to give 'life', 'eternal life' (6.33; 10.28). What is indicated is life-giving power, but this is indicated by the subject about whom the statement is made, not by the word life itself. Thus the gift of 'life' in 6.53 is a synonym for 'eternal life' and indicates a life which comes from another order of existence. Those who believe have 'life' (5.24; 20.31), but, more frequently, 'eternal life'

(3.15,16,36; 5.24; 6.47). The Father is the source of 'life' (5.26; 6.57–58) as life-giving power, and Jesus, who was sent by the Father, has been given life-giving power (5.25–26; 6.57–58). As far as the world is concerned, Jesus is the life (1.4; 11.25; 14.6). The life revealed in Jesus is the light of the world, judging the world, dividing men according to their response to the revelation (8.12). His coming was to give life (6.33; 10.10,28), through the giving of the life-giving Spirit (4.10–11; 7.37–39). Jesus' words are life-giving (4.50 (51),53; 6.68) and are related to the activity of the Spirit (6.63). His words are self-witness and concern the giving of his 'flesh', which, like the giving of 'himself', denotes the giving of himself to death in order that the world may live (6.51). Only by this act was he able to give the Spirit to believers (7.37–39; 16.7).

> The suggestion that Jesus' self-giving is to be understood in terms of his *psuchē* as distinct from his *zōē*, that is, in terms of his human life as distinct from his divine life, is nothing but the failure to take the incarnation seriously. A major text in support of this hypothesis is John 14.19, 'because I live you will live also'. In both instances the verb *zaō* is used. But Jesus uses the present tense of himself while he speaks of the disciples in the future tense. 'Because I live' is thus said to indicate the eternal nature of Jesus' divine life as the basis of the believers' future life. This is to miss the point. Of course it is Jesus' life that guarantees the future life of the believer. In its context John 14.19 refers to the resurrection situation when the disciples will see him again. Thus 'because I live' means 'because, being raised from the dead, I live ...'. For John the incarnation does not imply a doctrine of two natures, one human and one divine, because he asserts 'the Word became flesh' and he has taken this seriously. It is the risen Jesus who is the foundation of the believer's life. He is 'the resurrection and the life'. Resurrection and life flow from his risen life.

The character of the life given to believers was revealed in Jesus and may be described in terms of his self-giving love for the world or, more especially, for 'his own'. The gift of life is made effective in the lives of believers through the gift of the spirit (1.12f.; 3.5f.; 6.63) who inspired the apostolic witness (15.26–27) and creates the new love manifest in believers, so that they stand in judgement over against the false life of the world, just as the revelation of the life in Jesus condemned the Jews (5.39).

Not all references to 'eternal life' emphasize the present. The problem of physical death is not answered by this emphasis. Even those who have eternal life must experience physical death. But Jesus' life, which conquered death in the resurrection, is the basis of the believer's hope of resurrection (14.19).

More important for future eschatology is 5.29, which speaks of resurrection and judgement in terms reminiscent of Daniel 12.2. In this passage there is a double emphasis (as in the Lazarus sign) and again the themes of resurrection and life are linked.

Firstly, in 5.25 Jesus speaks of the spiritually dead who may now experience life through faith. Secondly, in 5.28 he speaks of the future, as the absence of 'and now is' (which occurs in 5.25) and the addition of 'all in the tombs' (which does not occur in 5.25) indicates. Reference here is to the general resurrection of the physically dead in the future, and 5.29, expressed in terms of Daniel 12.2, confirms this. Thus there is an inseparable connection between the present personal experience of salvation and the future general resurrection, as also in 6.39–40,44,54; 12.48; 11.25.

Bultmann attributes the future eschatological emphasis to an ecclesiastical redactor who has also added the sacramental emphasis, chapter 21 and certain tendencies in the direction of the Synoptics. But this view concerning eschatology and the sacraments lacks evidence and appears to arise from Bultmann's own theological views.

Jesus is the truth (14.6)

Truth is given definitive meaning in Jesus' words 'I am the truth'.

In the Old Testament, for example Psalm 119, and in the Qumran texts, truth and Word are identified with the Law.

Where Judaism asserted that the Law was truth, John declares that the truth revealed in Jesus is personal. The glory revealed in him was 'full of grace and truth' and is contrasted with the Law, 1.17. This development is related to the understanding of

Jesus as the Word. Jesus is the truth and the Word which he speaks from the Father is truth.

The coming of the truth in Jesus brought about a new situation (4.23–24). Genuine worshippers were now to come to God through Jesus, the revelation of God. Through faith in him believers receive the Spirit. Jew and gentile alike are called to believe in Jesus. The truth revealed is about God and concerns his faithfulness and love for the world, manifest in Jesus' mission into the world. The truth is that he is a saving God (as in Exodus 34.6). But in John this faithfulness is seen to break the boundaries of nationalism and is expressed in terms of God's universal love which opens up the way of salvation. The truth about God is that he is the giver of life, and this is expressed in terms of love. This universal love stands in judgement over against the nationalistic Jewish view of God. The judgement of the world continues through the gift of the Spirit who brings a new life to believers, vindicating Jesus' claim to have come from God, bringing the gift of new life (16.8ff.).

The truth in Jesus also concerns man because the true life of man is revealed in the incarnate Word. This is brought out especially in the sayings about the true bread and true drink. The true life for man comes from knowledge of the truth, the one who is true, who reveals the life of God, and gives life after the character of God's life to man. The revelation of this life in Jesus is the judgement of the world, revealing men's efforts to have life as falsehood.

Thus the truth is: the true life of God (1.4)
the true life for men (8.12)
saving truth (8.32)
in Jesus (14.6)
communicated by the Spirit (16.13)
received by those who do the truth (3.21)
who come to Jesus, believe in him (6.35)

Not all uses of truth in John have great theological significance. The terminology is also used straightforwardly to mean 'actually', 'truly'. The 'truth' and 'righteous' can be used to the same effect as in 8.16 and 5.30 (cf. also 7.24; 17.25; 16.8,10), and this indicates the underlying influence of the Hebrew

> *emunah*, which has a meaning which overlaps the Greek words for truth and righteousness.

Jesus is the true vine (15.1,5)

The true vine stands over against the false vine. Israel's apostasy is suggested by the use of this Old Testament imagery, and Jeremiah 2.21, in the Greek version, has a close parallel.

> The theme of Israel as God's vine is common in the Old Testament, (Hos. 10.1; Ezek. 15.1–8; 19.10ff.; Ps. 80.8–16). In later Judaism the vine was used as a symbol for the Messiah (2 Baruch 39.7; and Ps. 80.14 in Greek) and also for the Law (Sirach 24.17, 23ff.).

Jesus is God's vine, not Israel, whose apostasy is indicated in terms of the branches which do not abide in the vine. Thus Jesus constitutes the new, true Israel. Those who abide in Jesus (the vine), in his words, not those who abide in the Law, have life and will never hunger or thirst (cf. John 6.35), but those who come to Wisdom (Law) are even now hungry and thirsty (Sirach 24.17–24; see also p. 97f. below).

The true vine is Jesus, the Son of Man (cf. Ps. 80.16–17), who represents the true Israel of God. He constitutes those who abide in him as true Israelites (1.47). Consequently in this saying Jesus stands over against Israel and the Law.

CONCLUSION

Jesus' self-revelation draws attention to the christological basis of revelation. His eternal being is asserted in terms of the absolute use of 'I am', the significance of which is elsewhere spoken of by designating him as 'the Word' and 'the Unique Son'. But the character of the eternal being is spoken of in the symbolic self-designations. Symbols, drawn from the Old Testament which there referred to Israel and the Law, are now used christologically, indicating the situation (of conflict with Judaism) for which the Gospel was written.

> The 'I am' statements (cf. Isa. 43.10, etc.) are similar in form to the egoistic address in which Wisdom calls men to herself

and offers herself to men as the way of life. The similarities between Wisdom's kerygma and Jesus' discourses in John should be noted (Proverbs 1.21; 8.1ff.; Sirach 24). Attention has already been drawn to the cosmological function of Wisdom in relation to the Prologue. The divine origin of Wisdom heightens her kerygmatic stature. Who can afford not to listen? This is also the effect of John's Logos (Word) Christology which is to be compared with the kerygmatic appeal in Hebrews 2.1–4 following the Christology based on Wisdom (Heb. 1), especially noting 'radiance' (*apaugasma*) in 1.3 and Wisdom 7.26.

Wisdom offers herself to men as food and drink (Sirach 24.21; Prov. 9.5; cf. John 6.35,51,53, etc.). She promises to pour out her spirit upon those who will listen (Prov. 1.23; cf. John 7.37ff.). She calls men to listen and claims to dispense life (Prov. 3.18; 8.1ff.,25; Sirach 24.19). Her main theme is life (Prov. 8.35), 'the path of life' (Prov. 2.19, 5.6; 10.17; 15.24), 'the fountain of life' (Prov. 10.11; 13.14; 14.27; 16.22), 'the tree of life' (Prov. 11.30; 13.12; 15.4), which is Wisdom (Prov. 3.18). John also teaches that 'life' is a grace dependent on a relation with the living God. But in Proverbs and Sirach 'life' is the good things of life, length of days (Prov. 3.16; 28.16), a good name (Prov. 10.7; 22.1), riches and honour (Prov. 22.24) and possessions are a gift from God (Prov. 10.22), but death is a calamity for the wicked.

In the book of Wisdom 'life' becomes 'immortality' under Hellenistic influence (Wisdom 1.5; 15.3). But even in Proverbs 'life' points beyond earthly existence (Prov. 11.6,21; 13.6). In the saying 'whoever finds me finds life' (Prov. 8.35 cf. Sirach 4.12) the equation Wisdom=life is made because Wisdom does not come as an 'it' but as a person, a summoning 'I', as the form in which the Lord (Yahweh) makes himself present and in which he wishes to be sought by men. 'Whoever finds me finds life.' Only the Lord (Yahweh) can speak this way (von Rad). In the Fourth Gospel it is the summoning 'I' of Jesus, who claims that those who find him find life (John 11.25; 14.6; 17.3).

4 The Revelation of the Glory

John's use of 'glory' and 'glorify' is basically the same as that in the Old Testament and the Synoptics. This language describes the visible manifestation of God's presence as an object of sight. The Old Testament looks back to certain partial manifestations and forward to the complete manifestation in the future (Isa. 40.5; Sirach 45.3). In the Synoptics, with one exception, the 'glory' is reserved for the future coming of the Son of Man (Mark 8.38; 10.37; 13.26). The exception is the transfiguration, which Luke describes in terms of 'glory' (Luke 9.32), but Mark speaks of in terms of 'transfiguration' or 'metamorphosis' (Mark 9.2).

The 'transfiguration' of Jesus is reminiscent of what is described of Moses in Exod. 34.29ff. (cf. 2 Cor. 3.18) using the terminology of 'glory'. Luke is closer in terminology to Exodus than Mark, who does not use 'glory' but instead speaks of 'transfiguration'. This word betrays a pagan religious background, but is interpreted in terms of the idea of 'glory' in the Old Testament. In 2 Corinthians 3.18, Paul combines the languages of 'glory' and 'transfiguration'. The language of 'transfiguration' suggests that pagan readers were in view. The language of 'glory' in John confirms the Jewish situation for which it was written.

In the Old Testament, the Synoptics, John and common Greek use, the meaning of 'glory' overlaps with 'honour' or 'praise'. In fact, the Greek word for 'honour' is sometimes used in the New Testament to translate the Hebrew 'glory'. This usage accounts for ten of the nineteen uses of 'glory' in John. But the verb 'to glorify' is never used in this sense except in the appendix in 21.19, which is modelled on 12.33 and 18.32. This usage is not consistent with the rest of the Gospel, where the verb 'to honour' is used in this sense and 'glorify' has a more important theological meaning.

In John while there is a certain ambiguity about the meaning of the noun 'glory', the verb 'glorify' is used only with the Father, Son or Spirit as the subject of the verb used in the active voice, and when the Father and Son are said to be glorified (passive), it is the one by the other or by the Spirit. In this way Jesus is made the focal point of God's glory. This is characteristic of John's christological concentration.

John's distinctive interpretation is also to be seen in the relation between the verbs 'to glorify' and 'to lift up' or 'exalt', as in 12.23,31 and 3.14; 8.28; 12.34. This linguistic connection is to be found in the Old Testament (Exod. 15.2; Isa. 33.10; 52.13, etc.). It also relates to the New Testament teaching that God casts down the proud but 'exalts' the humble, for example Matthew 11.23, which is also expressed in terms of the sequence of the humiliation of Jesus which preceded his exaltation to the right hand of the Father (Acts 2.33; 5.31; (7.55)). But for John the glory of the Son of Man did not follow his humiliation. The true glory is to be seen in that humiliation, especially in the event of the cross. The lifting up or exaltation of Jesus is on the cross and it is this which makes the distinctive meaning of John's understanding of glory.

GLORY AND SIGNS

Raymond Brown has divided the Gospel into the Book of Signs (1.19—12.50) and the Book of Glory (13.1—20.31). The description recognizes the concentration of signs in chapters 1—12 but overlooks the post-resurrection signs and 20.31, which implies that the whole Gospel is in some sense a book of signs. The title Book of Glory for chapters 13—21 overlooks the fact that the majority of references to 'glory' occur in chapters 1—12. John also speaks of the revelation of Jesus' glory through his signs (2.11). Thus the whole Gospel could be called a book of glory.

The first sign at Cana of Galilee concludes with the statement that Jesus manifested his glory in this sign with the consequence that his disciples believed in him (2.11). This manifestation of glory is presupposed in all of the signs. But not everyone saw the glory in the signs (12.37–43). The Jewish authorities could acknowledge that Jesus performed signs (11.47) but they tended to be sceptical (9.18). Inasmuch as they acknowledged the signs, they saw them as mere miracles. The crowd of 6.26 also failed to see the feeding sign as anything but a mere miracle. Immediately after this sign they demanded a sign from heaven as a demonstration of Jesus' authority (6.30). The repeated demand for a sign shows the failure to see Jesus' miracles as signs of his authority (2.18; 4.48; 6.30). It was a failure to see the glory manifest in the signs.

Seeing signs as a way of coming to believe in Jesus is an often repeated theme (2.23–25; 3.2; 4.48; 6.2,14f.; 7.31; 9.16; 10.41–42; 12.18–19,42). But it becomes apparent that the faith described here, though certainly a positive development from the official Jewish rejection of the significance of Jesus' signs, is nevertheless always suspect, inadequate (2.23ff.; 6.14; 7.31; 12.42). This also is one implication of 4.48, 'Except you see signs and wonders you will not believe'.

In John, the signs are seen in a different way by different people at different times. The signs were seen by some as mere miracles indicating nothing of Jesus' significance. But there were many who saw in the signs something of the glory which was revealed there. They came to believe in Jesus, in some sense, as a prophet, even *the* prophet, or perhaps the Messiah (2.23–25; 3.1ff.; 6.14,15; 11.47–48). But this was to misconstrue the nature of the glory and to misunderstand Jesus in terms of a this-worldly kingdom, to give him a role which he renounced in no uncertain terms (18.36). Thus the faith of the crowds proved to be fickle because it was largely based on misunderstanding. In the discourses, Jesus confronts and clarifies misunderstanding, as the discussion of the misunderstanding motif demonstrated.

Bultmann takes a negative view of the value of the miraculous signs in the Gospel because they invariably lead to misunderstanding. But this is to misconstrue the evidence. The fault does not lie with the signs but with men who fail to see the true nature of the glory revealed in Jesus' signs (2.23–25). The signs were intended to lead men to the one who could give them eternal life (6.68). The fact that men concentrated on the display of power, rather than the function and purpose of the power was not a fault inherent in the signs themselves. The word 'sign', in its history of meaning, indicates a miraculous event. For this reason, Jesus speaks of his 'works' rather than 'signs'. Only in 4.48; 6.26 does Jesus speak of signs, and there he is speaking of the views of others. His description, 'works', draws attention to one aspect of the tenfold witness to him (5.36; 10.25). 'Sign' is a description of the miracles from the point of view of onlookers. 'Works' is Jesus' own description of his miracles as witness to his relation with the Father.

To single out the 'signs' as the basis of misunderstanding would be to miss an important emphasis in the Gospel. Jesus' words are also misunderstood. In fact, throughout Jesus' ministry, the faith provoked, whether by sign or by discourse, proves to be inadequate. It is true that the faith dependent on sign alone is more inadequate than that which takes account of Jesus' words. Thus belief on the basis of Jesus' works is made the starting-point for those who are unable to accept his self-testimony (10.38; 14.11). But ultimately the scandal of Jesus' claims cannot be avoided because it is involved in the acceptance of his 'works'.

The glory manifest in the signs was sometimes overlooked and at other times misunderstood during Jesus' ministry. The level of misunderstanding varied and consequently the validity of faith varied, from the crowds whose faith was fickle, to the disciples who, though they had misunderstood the nature of Jesus' glory, had really committed themselves to following him. The failure which produced rejection and misunderstanding was not inherent in the signs, but in those who failed to see or misunderstood the glory revealed in them. This distinction is important because it takes account of the fact that at a later stage the signs, as much as the words of Jesus, are able to evoke full and authentic faith. What separates that time from Jesus' ministry is his glorification. It is this event which enabled men to see the true nature of the glory revealed in Jesus' signs.

THE GLORIFICATION OF THE SON OF MAN

The glorification of Jesus, the Son of Man, is John's way of expressing the nature of Jesus' kingship. The phrase the 'kingdom of God' occurs only in 3.3,5; and in chapters 1—12 Jesus is referred to as 'king' only in 1.50; 6.15; 12.13,15. But 'Son of Man' is used twelve times of Jesus in chapters 1—13 (and nowhere after this) to express Jesus' kingship. In chapters 18—19, Jesus is referred to as king twelve times and in 18.36, Jesus spoke of 'my kingdom' three times, making clear that his kingdom is not a political kingdom of this world. Only when Jesus' death was imminent did he accept the kingship ascription, because misunderstanding was ruled out by the situation. Prior to this, the nature of Jesus' kingship is shown through the Son of Man theme, thus bringing a corrective to bear on the misconceptions.

> 'Son of Man' is to be understood against the background of the creation 'myth' known to Israel. The first man was king of paradise, he was given dominion (Gen. 1.28). Primal kingship was the subject of a great deal of speculation, the wider background becoming apparent in Psalm 8; Ezekiel 28.1–19; Job 15.7f. The kings of Israel were understood as successors to the primal king and the restoration of paradise was promised through one of them (Gen. 3.15). When Davidic kingship replaced the first man, dominion was interpreted in a nationalistic sense rather than in terms of mankind. But some features of the original dominion of man were retained. King of the restored paradise would be 'the seed of the woman' (Gen. 3.15; Isa. 7.14; 9.6f.; 11.1–16) suggesting the title 'the son of the woman', which is an alternative to Son of Man in 1 Enoch 62.5(29); and is suggested also in Revelation 12.13 and in the Hymn scroll of Qumran, 1 QH 3.7ff.
>
> In the Apocalyptic literature, the Messianic hope was developed eschatologically, but the Son of Man had long been a title for the king (Ps. 8.4–5; 80.17). In Daniel 7, the Son of Man is Israel's future king, a supernatural deliverer, who would restore dominion to the rightful people, Israel, whom he represented. The original myth spoke of man's dominion, but this has been nationalized, becoming Israel's dominion. Inasmuch as other kingdoms are represented by animals, the form of the original myth is preserved. The Son of Man represents the human, Israel. The form of the myth is preserved also in that the beasts arise from the sea, reminiscent of the Lord's battle with the deep in the creation myth, Psalm 98 and 4 Ezra 11.1ff. The judgement and kingship theme of Daniel is merged with the pre-existent revealer of heavenly secrets in 1 Enoch and 4 Ezra.

Son of Man, according to all of the Gospels, is Jesus' choice as a self-designation. In John the title is used only by Jesus except where the crowd asks a question about the Son of Man in response to a statement made by Jesus (12.34). But there are differences between the portrayal of the Son of Man in John and in the Synoptics.

> Although 'Son of Man' is only used in the Gospels in the New Testament, Paul's interpretation of Jesus as the last Adam, the second Man, the inaugurator of a new humanity, might be a development from it. To gentiles, 'Son of Man' would have been meaningless. In the gentile situation, the early Church soon lost the significance of the title.

The Son of Man sayings in the Synoptics are commonly divided into three groups, representing three phases

1. Earthly ministry,
2. Passion prediction,
3. Prediction of future glory.

But, for John, the Son of Man is the supernatural heavenly king, revealer of heavenly secrets. The three phases of the Synoptics imperceptibly merge because the glory was to be seen in the whole of Jesus' life, but especially in his exaltation to the Father by way of the cross (3.14; 8.28; 12.23,31,34). This event is the key for the recognition of glory in the life of Jesus. Thus this event is singled out and spoken of as the glorification of the Son of Man. Only after this event was it possible for the eyewitnesses to look back, in the reflection of faith created by Jesus' glorification, and become aware that throughout his life, in every way, including the signs, they had seen his glory (2.22; 12.16). From this perspective, the nature of glory has taken on a new dimension. That is why, from this perspective, the signs may now provoke authentic faith. Jesus' glorification has changed man's situation. The change can be accounted for in three ways: (i) what Jesus achieved for man in his glorification, (ii) what was revealed about the nature of glory in his glorification, (iii) and the coming of the Spirit made possible by his glorification (7.37–39; 16.7).

The theme of the exaltation and glorification of the Son of Man is stated for the first time in an unusual form in 1.51. Nathaniel's confession, 'Rabbi, you are the Son of God, you are the king of Israel', was evoked by Jesus' miraculous knowledge. Jesus' response indicates the inadequacy of the confession which names him 'rabbi', 'Son of God' and 'king of Israel'. In this context, the latter two titles are synonyms for Messiah (compare 1.45). 'Rabbi' indicates that Nathaniel regards Jesus as a purely human Messiah (cf. 3.2). Typical of Johannine irony, those who know that Jesus is the Word made flesh can understand that in a man, a rabbi, we meet the eternal Son of God. But this is the hidden meaning understood in retrospect. Jesus' words take account of the confession in the purely messianic sense. Nathaniel's faith will soon be based on a greater event. The heaven will be opened and there he will see the Son of Man as the central figure worshipped, not only by men (9.36), but also all angels (cf. Heb. 1.6). The time of this event is the exaltation of the Son of Man to heaven by way of the cross. That exaltation is understood as the enthronement of the heavenly king (17.5).

> Some commentators interpret Jesus as Jacob's ladder (Gen. 28.12), the way by which heavenly traffic passes to earth. This interpretation has no support from the Gospel. Contact with the heavenly realm is not dependent on angelic messengers. Further, the words 'You will see the heaven opened', as in Rev. 4.1, set the scene in heaven where the Son of Man is seen enthroned as heavenly king. This interpretation has the added merit of correcting Nathaniel's confession in its own terms. Instead of regarding Jesus as a human national king, Nathaniel will come to regard him as the divine heavenly king, enthroned by way of the cross.

The Son of Man, heavenly king, enthroned by way of the cross (3.13; 6.62) is a reassertion of the universality of the kingdom of God over against the nationalistic messianic hope confessed by Nathaniel. The cross cuts through nationalism. Thus in John, Jesus tells that 'the Son of Man must be lifted up' (3.14; 12,23,34), (whereas Mark reports 'the Son of Man must suffer ...'—Mark 8.31) to exert his universal lordship, drawing all men to himself (12.32). In this way, the kingdom was opened to all believers. For the Father, who draws men (6.44), draws them through the uplifted Son of Man (5.19; 12.32). It is the love of God revealed in Jesus that draws men (cf. Jer. 38.3). John's use of the Son of Man theme highlights Jesus' universal significance.

The exalted Son of Man king is also judge (5.27). The use of 'Son of Man' without 'the' draws attention to Daniel 7.13ff.

The judgement has both a present (5.25) and future aspect (5.29) (cf. Daniel 12.2). The giving of life and condemnation are experienced in the present. Those who believe have life and those who do not are condemned already (3.18,36). In the future, resurrection to life is promised to believers but wrath continues for those who do not believe (5.29).

'Glory' in the Old Testament was understood as the visible manifestation of the divine presence and was associated especially with the temple. Jesus is the new temple (2.21) in whom the divine glory was to be seen (1.14). The glorification of Jesus enabled the eye-witnesses of Jesus' life to become aware that they had seen Jesus' glory throughout his ministry.

John does not develop a 'Son of Man' Christology because this designation can only be understood in relation to the teaching about 'the unique Son' (*monogenēs*) who is the Word of the Father. As the (Logos) Word, his revealing activity is in focus, but the personal nature of the Word is emphasized, in his relation to the Father, by calling him 'the unique Son'. The Word, 'the unique Son', is himself divine and enjoys a unique relationship with God (the Father).

In the Prologue the Revealer is designated both as the Word and unique Son, but elsewhere is referred to only as 'the unique Son', or simply as 'the Son'. In this way the divine nature of the Revealer is clarified. 'The Word was divine' (1.1). The absence of the definite article (*theos* not *ho theos*) indicates that the meaning is 'divine' as distinct from 'the Word was with God' (*ho theos*). The definite article (*ho*) indicates that the reference is to a particular divine person elsewhere designated 'the Father' (1.18). Thus in the beginning the Word, the unique divine Son, was with God the Father.

The Prologue speaks of the creation of all things by the divine Word and his entry into created and historical existence (1.3,14). Elsewhere in the Gospel Jesus refers to this entry as his mission from the Father. But John 1.14 goes beyond the statements about the historic mission of the Son and proclaims the incarnation of the Word. The Word, the divine agent in creation, who as the unique Son shares the divine nature with the Father, became flesh. John asserts the actuality of this event. It is not said that the Word appeared, nor that the Word took a body, but the Word became flesh. 'Flesh' is the description of man in his weakness and corruption, man as fallen, whose existence leads on inexorably to death (existence unto death). When the Word became flesh he accepted the sentence of death which marks the existence of all flesh (Isa. 40.6–8). The real humanity of Jesus is not in question in the Gospel. What is questioned is the assertion that, in the frailty of the man Jesus, men encounter the eternal divine Word. But the glory of the divine is not incompatible with the frailty of human existence. The affirmation of the incarnation remains paradoxical because the divine Word is Spirit (John 4.24), eternal life-giving power (John 6.63).

John 1.14 is a crux verse. It makes three major claims:

1. Jesus' glory was seen, 'we beheld' (aorist tense), not 'we now see'. We who believe and were eye-witnesses, in the reflection of faith, are aware that 'we beheld his glory'. The glory was revealed in historical actions, was visible to sight and was recognized by those who believed.

2. The origin of the glory is the Father whose glory is expressed in his unique Son. What was seen was 'the glory of the unique Son of the Father ...', whom to see was to see the Father (1.18; 14.9), because the Son's glory comes from the Father (17.22).

3. The character of the glory is described '... full of grace and truth'. John sets out to make clear the character of the divine glory from the beginning. It is the self-giving love of Jesus, who gave himself for the world, and this is understood as the self-giving of God (3.16; cf. 1 John 4.7ff.). The glory is revealed in humiliation, suffering and unswerving faithfulness to the world which refused to know him. Despite this love, outside of faith it can only be said, 'You will die in your sins (8.24), for the exaltation of the Son of Man condemns as well as gives life. Through this event, the world is judged (12.31).

Thus John first states that the glory was seen, he then indicates the origin of the glory and finally expounds the character of glory.

DISCIPLESHIP AND GLORY

The glorification of the Father in the Son continues in Jesus' disciples (15.8). The character of the life once revealed in him is now revealed in them (17.10; 13.35). The glory the Father gave to Jesus is now given to them (17.22). This new glorification is realized through the power of Jesus' words (17.8) and the coming of the Spirit (16.14). The glorification of the disciples is a consequence of Jesus' glorification, so that while the disciples will manifest the same character of life, their lives are not a repetition of Jesus' unique work. Just as Jesus, having faithfully revealed the Father, entered his heavenly glory (17.5), so it is Jesus' prayer that those who are faithful in the world may share his heavenly glory (17.22). Hence glory points beyond this worldly life to the situation where we shall be with him.

John 17 has been called Jesus' High Priestly prayer. But John nowhere depicts Jesus as High Priest. It is rather the description of Jesus as our Advocate (Paraclete) with the Father (1 John 2.1 cf. John 14.16). The structure of the prayer can be set out as follows:

Jesus prays for 1. His glorification 1–5.
2. His first disciples 6–19.
3. Those who believe through their Word 20–26.

1. *Jesus prays for his glorification* (1–5)
The prayer reveals the critical nature of Jesus' glorification (his crucifixion and resurrection) as the event about to take place. In this event, through which Jesus returns to his heavenly glory (17.5) the Father is glorified, his character is revealed (17.1). Jesus' love for his disciples is the manifestation of God's love for the world. To know him is to know the Father. In this section, where Jesus' relationship with the Father is in view, Jesus speaks of the 'Father' and refers to himself as 'the Son', 'your Son' (17.1,5). Jesus' relation with the Father is also stressed in the use of Father in 17.21,24.

2. *Jesus prays for his first disciples* (6–19)
Jesus' relationship with his disciples is spoken of in terms

of his revelation to them. They are the men given to him by the Father. They had once belonged to the world but have been separated from it because Jesus revealed the Father's name to them and gave them the Father's Word. Consequently they had come to believe in him as the one sent by the Father. Jesus had kept them safe (except Judas). Now he is to leave them and he foresaw the danger that they would fall back into the immoral power of the world. Hence Jesus prayed for them, not for the world. His is not an anti-world attitude. Ultimately his concern for them is the expression of his concern for the world.

Jesus is glorified in the disciples because he has given them the Word and they have kept it. Now that he is to leave them he does not ask for their removal from the world. He asks that they shall be kept from the power of the evil one.

In this section Jesus refers to the Father as 'Holy Father' (17.11). By this designation, Holy (*hagie*), he indicates the Father's separation from the world. This title issued in the context of the request that the Father should separate the disciples from the power of the world. 'Keep them in your name' (17.12); sanctify (*hagiason*), separate them by the truth (your Word) (17.17). Thus the prayer is negatively, 'Don't let them become one with the world'; and positively, 'Do make them one with us (Father and Son)' (17.11). Unity is expressed in keeping the Father's Word (that Jesus had given them) and being sent into the world as he had been sent (17.18). Thus being separated from the corrupting power of the world, they were made free to live for the world. But their separation from the world and unity with the Father and Son had been made possible only through Jesus' mission, his victory over the power of the world and his fulfilment of the Father's mission.

3. *Jesus prays for the continuity of believers* (20–26)

Through the witness of the first disciples, made effective through the revelation of the Father's name and the giving of the Father's Word, the possibility of believing continues in the world. Jesus prayed for all subsequent believers. But all, from then on, would believe on the basis of the Word of the first disciples. They too would be in danger of falling under the corrupting power of the world. Thus Jesus prayed that they also might be one with the Father and himself. This is a processional unity. Just as the Father was made known in Jesus, so Jesus would be made known in his disciples through the Word he had given them. The Word would not only be spoken by them, it would transform their lives. Hence believers are united to Jesus by his Word, and through his Word Jesus continues to confront the world in the 'proclaiming existence' (Brunner) of the believers.

The unity in view (17.11,21,23) is not primarily the unity of believers with each other. It is the unity of believers with Jesus (and hence the Father) through the Word he had given them. Everything depends on abiding in his Word. Hence the danger that they will fall back into the power of the world. In this section Jesus addresses the Father as 'Righteous (*dikaie*) Father' which has more the meaning of 'Faithful Father'. Everything depends on God's faithfulness. Because of the faithfulness of God, Jesus' revelation of the Father's name would issue in the disciples' awareness of the Father's love for them. But not only that, his love would be the reality by which they lived, and the reality the world would see in their lives. Hence the world would continue to be challenged to believe in Jesus as the one sent by the Father. What is more, God's faithfulness would ensure that the believers' lives were not destroyed. Beyond death they would be with Jesus, they would share in his eternal glory.

Concluding remarks: Jesus' revelation of the Father's name is the Father's Word that he gave to the disciples. It is the power which is to separate the disciples for their mission. But Jesus' prayer is a request that the name, the Word, should be effective. The Father's answer to this request is 'the other Paraclete', 'the Spirit of Truth', who takes Jesus' place and works to continue the effects of Jesus' presence. In this way the glory the Father gave to Jesus is given to and to be seen in the believers (17.22).

5 *Revelation and Christology*

Emphasis on the christological concentration in John throughout the preceding chapters makes it possible for this to be little more than a summary chapter, bringing together the christological material. Jesus of Nazareth was the eternal Word of God incarnate. His dignity and person are properly understood in these terms. But the designation 'Word' is primarily functional and tells us that God has spoken to us in Jesus. He is able to do this because Jesus is the eternal Word made flesh.

The personal relationship between the Father and the Word is better expressed by referring to the unique Son of the Father. The unique Son, like the Word, is said to be divine. The Son shares a unique and intimate relationship with the Father because he is loved by the Father (3.35; 5.20).

> Both Greek verbs, *phileō* and *agapaō*, are used of the Father's love for the Son, indicating that no difference of meaning can be attributed to these verbs in John.

The Father's love for the Son is expressed in showing the Son all that he does and giving all things into his hand. The Son's love for the Father is expressed in doing the will of the Father, doing only what he sees the Father doing, and speaking only what he hears from the Father. Thus to see the Son is to see the Father. The Father is revealed by the Son, and only by him (1.18; 3.32; 5.19,37; 6.46; 8.38; 14.6). The unique relationship between Father and Son is unequivocally stated again and again.

Jesus claims continuous vision of what the Father does (5.19), complete, not fragmentary, knowledge of the Father. The 'mutual' knowledge of the Father and the Son also highlights the unique relationship (10.15). The Father's knowledge of Jesus is to be understood in terms of his sending and empowering Jesus for his mission in the world. Jesus' knowledge of the Father is expressed in his obedience to the Father's will.

Jesus' vision of what the Father does, and his knowledge of the Father, reveal both his equality with (5.18), or oneness with (10.30), and his dependence on, the Father (5.19). The Son can do nothing of himself. His life is lived in obedience to the Father.

John, the Gospel which makes the most exalted claims concerning the dignity and person of Jesus as the incarnate Word, the unique Son, more than any of the other Gospels, asserts the absolute dependence of the Son on the Father. In fact, these two aspects are so stated that Jesus' dignity is wholly dependent on his obedience to the Father's will. For John, Father and Son are used in the sense of the two persons who are both divine, but where the relationship between the two is that of the dependence of the Son on the Father. Because of this, the Son's words and actions really do come from the Father.

In John, Jesus also makes the most exalted claims, 'Before Abraham was, I am'. Thus speaks the eternal Word incarnate. But his dignity and significance are only properly understood when the self-witness of Jesus is seen to be an indication of his significance for the world. Again and again this significance is revealed by symbols which show his self-giving service to bring life to the world.

John emphasizes the love of God revealed in Jesus. It is this that stands in judgement over the hatred in the world. He also mentions, without emphasis, that Jesus is the lamb of God who bears away the sin of the world (1.29,36), that Jesus gave himself for the life of the world (6.51), his life for his sheep (10.15), his life for his friends (15.13,14). But John does not explain in what manner the giving of Jesus' life brought life: at least there is an unexplained element. What is explained is that, through the event of the cross, the power of evil is broken and men are provoked to believe in God's act of love for them. John emphasizes this aspect of Jesus' work because it is as the new and greater revelation that Jesus supersedes the revelation of Judaism. This is the point John seeks to make clear.

The fullness of the divine glory revealed in Jesus is given definitive expression through his self-giving on the cross. The uplifting of the Son of Man, proclaimed king by the Father, demonstrates that the divine love is the most powerful force in the universe. The revelation of that love in the world produced the judgement of the world, bringing life to those who would receive it, but wrath to those who rejected it. The glorification of the Son of Man is the judgement of the world and a foretaste of the final judgement, which is also to be performed by the exalted Son of Man. Jesus' glorification is bound up with another event without which it cannot be understood. That event is the coming of the Spirit, made possible through Jesus' glorification (7.37–39;

16.7), and making the judgement of Jesus' glorification effective (16.8,14).

6 *Revelation and the Spirit*

John's treatment of the role of the Spirit in revelation presupposes the Old Testament and Jewish view that 'God is Spirit' (*pneuma ho theos*), John 4.24. This is a statement about the being of God, not an indication that he is a spirit being. Spirit is contrasted with man as flesh (John 1.12–13; Isa. 31.3; 40.6–8; 1 QH 4.20–22,29). This is the contrast between the eternal, universal God, in his life-giving power, with man in his weakness and corruption. Salvation for man does not come through the flesh but through the Spirit; salvation is of God (John 1.12–13).

In John 4.24 'God' (*ho theos*) refers to the Father (4.23) as in John 1.1, 'the Word was with God' (*ho theos*). It is also said that the Word was 'divine' (*theos*). In Johannine terms the Word also is 'Spirit' (without the definite article). But John also speaks of 'the Spirit' (1.33; 3.34; 7.39); 'the Holy Spirit' ((*to*) *pneuma to hagion*) (1.33; 14.26); 'the Spirit of truth' (14.17; 15.26; 16.13); 'the (another) Paraclete' (14.17,26; 15.26; 16.7). In these references the Spirit is spoken of as 'he'. He has a relation to the Father and the Son and personal functions such as teaching, leading, convicting, witnessing, are ascribed to him. Reference to the role of the Spirit in revelation presupposes this basic distinction between 'God is Spirit' and *the* Spirit who, like the Father and the Son (the Word), is divine.

> With these statements John, more than any other writer in the New Testament, presents us with the evidence which forced the Early Church, almost against its will, to formulate the doctrine of the Trinity.

The Spirit plays a significant role in the work of revelation. There was no effective revelation prior to the glorification of Jesus when the Spirit was given (7.39; 14.7,9; 16.30f.).

John 7.37–39 is to be interpreted christologically. It is Jesus who gives the Spirit. The 'inexhaustible spring' indicates that the life Jesus gives is eternal. It *is* NOT said that the believer becomes a source of the Spirit for others. Jesus makes the offer of water (7.37), which is to be punctuated: 'If any one thirsts let him come to me, and let him drink who believes in me.' (so Bultmann, p. 303; cf. John 6.35). This is followed by an appeal to Scripture to back up the claim (7.38) and the imminent gift of the Spirit, by Jesus to believers, is spoken of straightforwardly (7.39). The water from Jesus' side (19.34) may well symbolize the fulfilment of this saying.

During Jesus' ministry, the activity of the Spirit is confined to Jesus. But Jesus is not understood simply as an inspired man. He is the Word made flesh, the unique Son, who experiences the Spirit fully and permanently (1.33; 3.34). He is the one who gives the Spirit (1.33; 4.10ff.; 7.37ff.).

During the 'Farewell Discourses' of chapters 14—16, Jesus speaks of the activity of the Spirit in the post-glorification situation. The references fall into four fairly self-contained passages. Two titles, 'Paraclete' and 'The Spirit of Truth', occur only here in the Gospel and '*the* Holy Spirit' occurs only here in its full Greek form. But the teaching is consistent with the Gospel as a whole. It serves to clarify Jesus' relationship with the Spirit and to explain the development of faith and knowledge after Jesus' glorification.

It has been argued that 'the Paraclete passages' are insertions from a source. But this theory runs into the problem of all source theories in John, the apparent unity of the Gospel in style. From a theological point of view, these passages develop and unify themes in the Gospel as a whole. Further, if the passages come from a source, why were they not inserted in one block of material instead of a number of fragments?

The titles Spirit of Truth and Paraclete remain somewhat enigmatic. Some background understanding is provided by the Qumran texts. Here the 'Holy Spirit' is identified with 'the Spirit of Truth' and is opposed to 'the Spirit of Falsehood'. This antithesis is linguistically close to 1 John 4.6, but no antithesis of this sort occurs in the Gospel. Much of the vocabulary of the Qumran texts is similar to that of the Gospel, but there is nothing that could be translated 'Paraclete'.

The background to John's use of 'Paraclete' remains unknown, and even the question of a precise translation finds no unanimous answer. 'Advocate' is suggested by the passages which deal with the persecution of the disciples (15.8–25; 16.2–3,32). But the Paraclete is the one who convicts the world (16.8–11); he is the witness from Jesus who is on trial (15.26). This is a recurring theme (5.31–40; 8.13–19; 18.19–24,33–38). The witness of the Paraclete vindicates Jesus and convicts the world. But 'Advocate' is the correct translation of 1 John 2.1 and there it is applied to Jesus.

'Comforter' is suggested by the contexts dealing with Jesus' announcement of his departure to his sorrowing disciples (16.6–7). But the theme of judgement appears in 16.8ff. Bultmann describes the Spirit as 'the power within the Church which brings forth both the knowledge and proclamation of the Word'. The Paraclete is the prophetic Spirit, the inspirer of the testimony to Jesus through which the world is judged. Thus 15.26–27 refers to the one inspired witness of those who had been with Jesus from the beginning.

Jesus is the original Paraclete (1 John 2.1) and the Spirit is referred to as 'another Paraclete' (14.16). Thus the Paraclete has functions which parallel those of Jesus. Both Jesus and the Paraclete:

(*a*) Are sent by the Father (5.30; 8.16,42; 13.3 and 14.16; 15.26).
(*b*) Are recognized only by believers (1.10,12; 8.14,19; 17.8 and 14.17).
(*c*) Teach and lead believers into the truth (7.16f.; 8.32,40ff. and 14.26; 16.13).
(*d*) Do not represent themselves (7.16f.; 12.49f.; and 16.13).
(*e*) Bear witness to Jesus and convict the world of its sin (8.14; 3.20; 7.7; and 15.26; 16.8).

The parallelism is impressive but one difference is clear. The Paraclete is subordinate to Jesus. Jesus' witness to himself is paralleled by the Paraclete's witness to Jesus. If the Paraclete is sent by the Father, it is at Jesus' request (14.16) and he is sent in Jesus' name (14.26), or even sent from the Father by Jesus (15.26; 16.7). The Paraclete is known only by those who believe in Jesus (14.17) and his activity is completely Christ-centred (14.26; 15.26; 16.13–15). Just as Jesus' mission is dependent on the Father, the mission of the Paraclete is dependent on the Father and the Son. His revealing work originates with the Father, but is concerned with the Son who is manifest through the activity of the Paraclete.

In the first passage dealing with the Paraclete, a clear identification is made with the Spirit of Truth (14.16–17). The latter name indicates the divine nature of the Spirit. The Spirit is to be thought of in personal terms, distinct from the Father and Son. The Gospel personalizes the Spirit by using personal pronouns, 'he', ascribing to him functions such as leading, guiding, teaching. The name 'Spirit of Truth' also indicates that the Spirit takes Jesus' place, is sent by him, or sent in Jesus' name and his function is to bear witness to Jesus, to lead men to him and to him alone.

The Paraclete is sent to the disciples and the world does not recognize his presence (14.16–17). He consoles the disciples in their experience of abandonment in the world (14.18,23). But he is primarily the teacher (14.20), who reminds them of all that Jesus had said to them (14.26). This inspired remembrance is illustrated in the Gospel (2.22; 12.16). Both passages speak of the remembrance which occurred after Jesus' resurrection, after his glorification, through which the coming of the Paraclete was made possible (7.39; 16.7). Both passages relate the remembrance of words and events to the context of the Old Testament. It is remembrance within this context which brings out the true meaning which, until this point, had not been grasped. This is historical remembrance in the context of salvation history, and involves a new understanding. At the time of Jesus' departure, the disciples were not ready to hear what he had to tell them (16.12). Thus the Spirit of Truth came to guide them into the truth (16.13), that is, to Jesus (14.6). The activity of the Spirit is to make known the true significance of Jesus (16.13ff.).

What has been said applies primarily to the eye-witness believers. Only they could be reminded of what they had seen and heard. But the Spirit is given to all believers. All believers experience the witness of the Spirit to Jesus. For those who are not eye-witnesses of the Word, the witness of the Spirit is inseparably linked with the inspired eye-witness testimony (15.26–27). The Gospel of John is itself such inspired eye-witness testimony.

The world does not experience the Paraclete (14.17), but does encounter the inspired witness of those who were with Jesus from the beginning of his ministry (15.26–27). Thus the apostles have a unique place in salvation history. Their witness is the source of the Church's proclamation, so that the witness, which continued the effect of Jesus' coming (3.19ff.) persistently brings the world under judgement (16.8–11). The proclamation is also expressed in the life of the community, where it is manifest in brotherly love (13.35) or a 'proclaiming existence' (Brunner). While Jesus gave the command to love and his life manifests the norm, the Spirit gives the power to fulfil the norm of Christian conduct. The new life brought by the Spirit is characterized by love and it condemns the false way of life of the world. In this way, the rejection of the proclamation is exposed (9.39ff.; 15.22ff.). The world is exposed in its sinfulness and Jesus is proclaimed as vindicated. The verdict at Jesus' trial is reversed. The accuser becomes the accused and the world is declared guilty. Jesus' vindication (resurrection) is the foundation of this reversal. Because Jesus' death is a vindicated death, the prince of this world is condemned, and the world has the opportunity to believe (n.b. 16.8–11).

The vindication of Jesus is the revelation of the judgement of the world. The world is brought into contact with the reality of coming judgement. The Spirit announces the coming events (16.13). While recognizing the significance of what Jesus has achieved, John's eschatology remains oriented towards the future. The time is yet to come when the act of judgement, which is already a reality, will be fully realized (5.28–29). For the present, the Paraclete, at work in the apostolic life and witness of the Church, exposes the sin of the world and announces the vindication of Jesus and the certainty of coming judgement, because the prince of this world has already been judged.

There is no mention of the Spirit in chapters 13 and 17. In these chapters, Jesus and his word are the focal points. Jesus' life provides the disciples with an example to follow (13). But following is neither automatic nor easy. Chapters 14—16 give assurance that they will not be alone in this task. Jesus' request to the Father in 14.16 is given no content. But the sending of the Paraclete is the Father's answer to that request. Chapter 17 indicates the nature of Jesus' request to which the Father responds by sending the Paraclete.

The request of Chapter 17 has three main parts:

(*a*) For Jesus' glorification (17.1–5).
(*b*) For the eye-witness believers (17.6–19).
(*c*) For those who believe on the basis of eye-witness testimony (17.20–26).

From the point of view of this discussion, the first part is relevant only because the request for the believers was precipitated by his imminent departure and the fulfilment of the request was dependent on his glorification.

On the point of departure, Jesus was concerned that his disciples, whom he had called out of the world and had kept by his Word, would fall back into the grip of the world. The revelation of God's character in Jesus had kept them while he was with them. Jesus then prayed that the Father would keep those to whom he had given God's Word, that they might remain true to the revelation. The request is that the lives of the disciples might be an expression of the Word of revelation that Jesus had given them. It is this Word which separated them for their mission and ensures a succession of believers. Kept, sanctified, made one with the Father through the Son, the disciples would fulfil their mission.

Jesus prayed also for those who would believe through the witness of his disciples. Those who believed on the basis of the witness would also be separated from the world and made one with the Father and the Son in the mission to the world. Thus the revelation once made in Jesus continues to have an effect in the world, not only through the eye-witnesses, but also in those who believed on the basis of their witness. Jesus' Word, transmitted by the disciples, separates believers for their mission in the world. But this presupposes that the Word is truly received and known. The Paraclete brings about the knowledge and proclamation of the Word. The Paraclete is at work in the response to the revelation. Without his work, the revelation in Jesus would not be effective. Through his work the believing eye-witness testimony to the words and works of Jesus arose as the basis of belief and proclamation down through the ages.

> Two other references to the giving of the Spirit deserve attention. Both are in symbolic form. 19.34 looks back to 4.10 and 7.38. Here, water represents the Spirit as life-giving power. Thus the character of life for the believer is the creation of the Spirit. 20.22 interprets the coming of the Spirit as a new creation in terms of Genesis 2.7. The emphasis is on the new quality of life brought by the Spirit, to be understood in terms of love. The coming of the Spirit is also the assurance that the mission, spoken of in 20.21, will be effective.

The teaching about the Spirit moves in the opposite direction to mysticism because the Spirit is experienced in the encounter with the Jesus of history or through the historical witness borne to him. The presence of the Spirit is not known in a growing awareness of the Spirit, but in a growing appreciation of the significance of Jesus. The Spirit has nothing to say about himself, but draws attention to Jesus. This is characteristic of the christological concentration in John. The inspired testimony of the eye-witnesses is the basis for the believer's life in the world. It is the basis of the continuing opportunity for the world to come to know the love of God in Jesus.

The Spirit gives expression to the outgoing mission of God to the world which is at the heart of John's understanding of the Trinity. Mission is an expression of the love which originates with the Father, is revealed in the Son and is made actual in the lives of the believers through the presence of the Spirit.

With our discussion of the role of the Spirit, we have come to the conclusion of the exposition of revelation in the person of Christ, the major emphasis of the Gospel. In fact, the discussion of the role of the Spirit forms a bridge with the second emphasis, the response to and experience of the revelation. We have already seen that John considers that the stages of response can only be understood by taking into account the coming of the Spirit at the glorification of Jesus. We have also noted that an analysis of the response needs to take account of the distinction between believing eye-witnesses and subsequent believers.

7 *The Response to the Revelation I—Faith*

THE WAY TO FAITH

Faith (understood activity) is the proper response to the revelation in Jesus. John's understanding of the revelation has determined his view of faith. Because the revelation occurred in history, the way of coming to faith is through normal historical experience, through seeing or hearing.

Six different verbal forms are used to express the activity of seeing. Bultmann is of the opinion that these forms are used without any difference of meaning being intended. A careful analysis proves this judgement to be correct. Of course the various forms do provide the appropriate tenses. Bultmann suggests a threefold use of the verbs of seeing which does not depend on the various verbs having different meanings. Seeing is understood as:

(*a*) the general perception of events;
(*b*) the perception of supernatural objects by certain people;
(*c*) the seeing of faith, which has the revelation in view.

According to this view, there are two types of seeing; firstly, physical sight and, secondly, the vision of faith. The vision of faith not only describes the apostolic eye-witness situation, but also the faith of the believing community. In general terms, this is also the view of C. H. Dodd. But the idea of faith as vision will not stand up to careful examination. It is excluded by 20.29 alone, where Jesus speaks of believers who have seen him, as well as those who have never seen him. Faith and sight are clearly distinguished.

The evidence of the Gospel indicates two ways of coming to faith, seeing and hearing. The way of sight was open only to Jesus' contemporaries. But not all who saw Jesus and his signs came to believe in him. While the eye-witnesses also heard Jesus' word, hearing that word continues to be possible, and faith comes now only through hearing (cf. Rom. 10.17).

In the Gospel there were those who:

(*a*) saw Jesus but did not believe in him;
(*b*) saw Jesus and came to believe in a superficial way;
(*c*) came to authentic faith after Jesus' glorification.

We are concerned with the place of sight where faith in Jesus was rejected and accepted during his ministry. Not all of those who saw Jesus and his signs came to believe in him. Why was this? 'Misunderstanding' is the recurring answer given by the Gospel. The Jews thought that they had life. They thought that they knew God. Because of this they rejected the gift of life and knowledge of God in Jesus. Their knowledge was based on the Scriptures, which they used in a proof-texting fashion to avoid facing the claims of Jesus' words and works (5.39,45). They ruled out the possibility that Jesus had a place in salvation history on various grounds. There is a need to distinguish the intellectual arguments (used to justify the rejection of Jesus) from the moral and spiritual causes of unbelief.

The intellectual arguments are shown to be rationalizations of rejection by their lack of inner consistency.

1. Because the signs were not designed as public demonstrations of power, there were those who doubted their reality (7.4; 9.18). Ultimately the reality of the miracles could not be denied and even the leaders acknowledged their occurrence, but without coming to believe in Jesus (11.47ff.). When the miracles were not denied, their significance could be misconstrued.

2. Arguments from Scripture were used to deny Jesus a place in salvation history.

(*a*) His origin (family) was known, but the origin of the Messiah was to be unknown (6.42; 7.27).
(*b*) His place of origin was wrong, Galilee, not Bethlehem as foretold (7.41f.,52).
(*c*) His origin was not known, but it was known that Moses came from God (9.29).

Typical of the Johannine irony, the reader is expected to know that the Jews did not know Jesus' Father, that Jesus did come from Bethlehem and that he had come from God.

(*d*) He broke Sabbath law, therefore could not have come from God (5.10ff.; 9.13ff.). But the Old Testament gave precedents for the performance of certain works on the Sabbath (7.21ff.). Jesus also argued that he did only what the Father was doing. God's creative works continued on the Sabbath (5.17f.). In this way Jesus challenged the Jews to see God's ultimate revelation and act in him. But he was considered to be a blasphemer because his claim to be God went beyond the limits of the Old Testament. In the face of the scandal caused by his self-testimony, Jesus appealed to the witness of his works (5.36; 10.31–39). His transparently good works should have demonstrated sufficiently that he had some place in salvation history (9.16). Those who rejected both Jesus' words and works did so because their standard of judgement was perverted.

The moral cause of unbelief can be described as false or perverted love. Love is directed to the wrong object, man chooses wrongly. The element of choice is prominent when love and hate are used together or when love is wrongly directed. Both characteristics appear in 3.19–21.

The first false love is love of the darkness rather than the light (3.19–21). The world rejected God's approach in the revelation of the light. The light is rejected because men prefer the world apart from God. They prefer their own evil actions to the change that accepting the judgement of the light would bring.

The second false love is love for the glory of man rather than the glory of God (5.41–44; 7.18; 8.50; 12.43); the choice of self-advancement and self-exaltation, of false greatness, greatness apart from God, opposed to God.

The third false love is love for one's own life rather than love for God or anyone else (12.25). The fact that this love leads to death indicates that it is opposed to faith, which leads to life.

Perverted love, expressed in these ways, is also the manifestation of the claim to possess life already. Hence the Jews were hostile towards anyone who threatened or called their possession into question. Jesus opposed and condemned their self-assurance because it prevented men from acknowledging his works and hearing his words (9.39–41). But those who seek to do God's will, who seek honour from God, will know the origin of Jesus' doctrine (7.17). Those who 'do the truth' will come to the light (3.21). From this standpoint, response to the revelation is to be seen as an indication of moral integrity, or the lack of it.

The rejection of Jesus resulted from a moral failure. False standards produced false judgements. John suggests that the moral perversion has a spiritual cause. Thus ultimately, the cause of unbelief is not intellectual argument nor moral perversion, because the false moral standards have a spiritual cause.

The spiritual cause of unbelief is stated, concerning both hearing and seeing. The statement concerning seeing is given to explain why the Jews failed to see the glory revealed in Jesus' signs (12.37ff.). Thus we have a situation where there were those who acknowledged that Jesus performed signs (miracles) but were not challenged to believe in him (11.47). This explains also the repeated demand for an authenticating sign (2.18; 6.30) by those who had seen Jesus' miracles. They had not recognized the glory in the signs which witnessed to Jesus' authority. The failure to see the glory in the signs prevented faith.

In John 12.37ff. there is a quotation from Isaiah 6.10. But the text has been altered so that the one who has blinded the Jews is clearly distinguished from the one who would heal them. John has also introduced the word translated 'He has blinded ...'. Only one interpretation fits the context, explains why the Jews failed to see the glory of Jesus' signs and believe, and is consistent with the theology of the Gospel.

'He', the prince of this world (12.31) has blinded the Jews so that Jesus may not heal them. The New Testament provides only two other passages where the word translated 'he has blinded' is used (2 Cor. 4.4 and 1 John 2.11). Both passages confirm the interpretation given. In 2 Cor. 4.4, it is 'the god of this world' who 'has blinded the minds of the unbelieving, that the light of the gospel ... should not dawn upon them'. Paul was dealing with the problem of unbelief. The fault did not lie with the gospel, but with Satan who had made people insensitive so that they would not believe. 1 John 2.11 states that the darkness has blinded the eyes of those who walk in the darkness. In the Gospel, the prince of this world is the power of darkness (12.31; 14.30; 16.11). Here also John draws attention to the blinding effect of walking in the darkness, to be overcome only by believing in the light (12.35ff.).

Thus in John 12.40, 2 Cor. 4.4 and 1 John 2.11, it is Satan who has blinded the eyes of unbelievers. This 'dualistic' interpretation is confirmed by the Qumran texts. The parallel there is important in view of the general affinity with the Gospel. Parallels are nowhere closer than with regard to the Johannine 'dualism'. The interpretation is also confirmed by John's understanding of the reason why hearing Jesus' words did not always lead to faith. This comes out especially in Jesus' discussion with the Jews in chapter 8.

The Jews did not hear Jesus' words because they were the children of the devil (8.43ff.). They were his children because they had adopted his standards. Their false standards were derived from listening to their father, the devil (8.38–44). They had false standards of truth, freedom, and life, because they had mistaken the devil for God. The Jews were divided by the word Jesus spoke to them (10.20ff.). Many of those who rejected Jesus claimed that he was demon-possessed. They asked those who were listening to Jesus, 'Why do you go on listening to him?' Thus we see that the rejection of Jesus involved the refusal to listen to him based on a reversal of standards. Falsehood was called truth, and the one whom God had sent was called demon-possessed. Hence, for them, the devil was God. Because of this they rejected the truth of the knowledge of God in Jesus and the freedom from sin, eternal life, which he came to bring. They rejected Jesus' word and were challenged by Jesus to take account of his works (10.38). Had they given heed to his works, their standards would have been changed. But their eyes were blinded, they were unable to accept and obey Jesus' word.

All of this seems to suggest that some men are the children of the devil and cannot believe, and that other men are Jesus' sheep and cannot help believing. But this is not the case. All men, including 'the twelve', were once in the darkness, in the world (15.19; 17.6,9f.,24). Are those who believe given to Jesus in such a way that they automatically believe? Is this what 6.37–65, especially verses 37,44,45,65, suggests? Are those who do not believe prevented from doing so by God?

Contrary to what may seem obvious, 6.39 is balanced by 6.40, indicating that the Father gives Jesus those who believe in him, and 6.44f., which asserts that only those the Father draws can come to Jesus, is balanced by 12.31f. The exalted Son of Man draws all men to himself. Only those the Father gives can come to Jesus (6.65). The Father gives all who believe because the coming of Jesus is God's gift to the world (3.16). Even though the past had been determined by falsehood and darkness, the coming of the truth, the light, brought the possibility of becoming sons of light for those who believed (12.36).

The coming of the Word made flesh made belief possible (3.19–21). During the ministry of Jesus, his signs had a limited effect (as did his words), producing a limited faith (2.23ff.), even among the leaders (12.42f.). When Jesus was lifted up, the power of evil was broken (12.31f.) and faith on a universal scale became possible. This possibility links Jesus' resurrection (2.22), his glorification (12.16) and the coming of the Paraclete (14.26; 16.7). In the eschatological moment all men are called to believe. Those who believe leave the darkness for the light, while those who refuse to believe definitively choose the darkness and are finally and irrevocably in the darkness (3.19ff.; 9.39ff.).

Hearing as a way to faith does not always have Jesus' words directly in view. The witness of those who believed through Jesus' words is also the means by which others may come to believe (1.7,37,40; 4.39,42; 9.27; 10.41–42; 12.17–18). The Word of the witnesses fares exactly as Jesus' own Word because it is fundamentally the same (15.20). But this depends on the witnesses being one with Jesus, faithfully transmitting his Word. Only in this way does the possibility of believing continue in the world (17.20).

Both seeing and hearing are important because here we have the dual ways to faith. Neither seeing nor hearing are significant in themselves. It was to those who saw or heard and believed that life was given. It is to those who hear and believe that life continues to be given (5.24).

THE WAY OF FAITH

There is a concentration on believing in chapters 1—12 where Jesus confronts the world with the challenge to believe. Some statistical comparisons show in John the importance of believing.

	JOHN 1–12	JOHN 13–21	JOHN TOTAL	PAUL	SYNOPTICS	1 JOHN	N.T. TOTAL
'to believe'	76	22	98	54	30	9	239
'faith'	0	0	0	142	24	1	244

John uses the verb because, in the New Testament, the noun 'faith' usually occurs in contexts dealing with faith and works as the way of salvation. This was not a live controversy for John. The Pastoral Epistles use 'faith' to indicate the content of faith. John chose 'believe' because it suited his understanding of the proper response to the revelation, and he was able to indicate the content of faith using the verb followed by that, 'believe that'.

The emphasis in John on believing is clear. In twenty-one chapters we have almost half of the uses in the New Testament and more than three times the total number of uses in the Synoptics. The idea of believing is also indicated by a number of symbolic parallels. The various symbols focus attention on an aspect of what is a complex response to the revelation in Jesus. Most of the references occur in discourse passages and deal with an aspect of authentic faith. In the few instances where these symbols are used in narrative passages there are indications of the limited nature of the response. Believers who had seen Jesus are distinguished from those who had not by the symbols used and also by the way the verb 'to believe' is used (17.20; 20.29).

From the symbols, certain aspects of what it means to believe may be outlined. Believing involves:

	NARRATIVE	DISCOURSE
1. *Perception, recognition, understanding*		
To see	1.14	1.39,46,51; 6.40,62; 11.40; 12.40; 14.7,17
To hear	4.42; 10.20	5.24,25,45; 8.43,47; 10.3,8,16,27
To remember	2.17,22; 12.16	14.26
2. *Decision*		
To come	1.39,46	3.20,21; 6.35,37,45,65; 7.37; 14.6
To receive or reject		1.5,11,12; 3.11,32,33; 5.43; 12.48; 13.20; 14.17; 17.8
To love or hate	(21.15,16,17)	3.19,20; 8.42; 12.25,43; 14.15,21,23,24,28; 16.27
To confess or deny	9.22; 12.42; 18.25,26	13.38
To follow	(1.37,38,40); 6.2	1.43; 8.12; 10.4,5,27; 12.26
3. *Dependence and obedience*		
To drink		4.13,14(6.35); 7.37
To eat		(6.35); 6.51,52
To be a disciple	9.27	8.31; 13.35; 15.8
To learn or be taught		6.45
To keep		8.51(52); 14.15,21,23,24,28
To abide		6.56; 8.31(12.46); 15.4,5,6,9,10
To serve		12.26
To worship	9.38	4.23,24

Some of the terms overlap from one group to another so that to hear and to worship can involve all three categories, and to follow can involve obedience as well as decision. Seeing and remembering are restricted to the situation of Jesus' ministry. Only those who had actually seen Jesus could remember, with new understanding, what their eyes had seen and their ears had heard. The new understanding was produced by Jesus' glorification and the coming of the Spirit.

John's use of the verb 'to believe' emphatically describes the response to the revelation. Thus neither Jesus nor the Father are said to believe, nor is the verb used in the Old Testament sense of the faithfulness of God. 'Believe' is used in a number of different grammatical constructions. An analysis of these highlights in John the meaning of belief.

1. The verb is used eighteen times with the indirect object of the person or words believed. This usage expresses the theme of

belief on the basis of witness which is so important in the Gospel. The focal point of the witness is Jesus. His self-testimony, with the witness of the Father in his works, is more important than the other witnesses who make up the tenfold testimony (5.31–39; 8.13–18). The witness of the works provides a transition (10.38; 14.11). But ultimately the scandal of Jesus' self-testimony cannot be avoided. All uses but one of this construction fall in chapters 1—12, where the tenfold witness to Jesus is borne (apart from 15.26–27; 19.35; 21.24). After Jesus' resurrection, the testimony of the eye-witnesses takes on new significance. John has used the cases reported in chapters 1—12 to illustrate the principle of witness, the importance of which, for future belief, is outlined in 15.26–27; 17.20ff.; 20.31.

Instances of this construction indicate believing Jesus (4.21; 5.38,46; 6.30; 8.31,45–46; 10.37–38); Jesus' words (2.22; 4.50; 5.47); Jesus' works (10.38 (14.11)); Him who sent Jesus (5.24); the Scriptures (2.22; 5.46–47; 12.38).

2. Characteristically John speaks of 'believing in'. Of the 47 uses of this construction in the New Testament 36 occur in the Gospel, 3 in 1 John, 3 in Acts. No other book has more than one use of this construction, which is peculiar to the New Testament. Jesus is always the person who is the object of belief, except in 12.44 and 14.1, which refer to the Father who sent Jesus. Thus John emphasizes the personal nature of belief using this construction.

'Believing in' is used in 1.12; 2.11,23; 3.16,18,36; 4.39; 6.29,35,40; 7.5,31,38,39,48; 8.30; 9.35,36; 10.42; 11.25,26,45,48; 12.11,36,37,42,44,46; 14.1,12; 16.9; 17.20. A different preposition is used in 3.15 and 20.31, but in the same sense. This is borne out by the parallelism between 3.15 and 3.16. In the case of 20.31, believing in Jesus' name is elsewhere spoken of (1.12; 2.23; 3.18), but never having life in his name. The parallelism, 'believing that', is balanced by 'believing in' and 1 John 5.13, modelled on John 20.31, uses the normal Johannine formula 'believing in'. In New Testament times, the two prepositions translated 'in' tended to overlap in meaning.

3. The verb is used absolutely (without a stated object) 28 times. But the context implies the object in all but 16 instances. In these

instances, which tend to fall in the discourses, 'believe' has the meaning of authentic Christian faith.

> The absolute use occurs in 1.7,50; 3.12,18; 4.41,42,48,53; 5.44; 6.36,47,64; 9.38; 10.25,26; 11.15,40; 12.39; 14.11,29; 16.31; 19.35; 20.8,25,29.

4. The verb is used followed by 'that', 'to believe that ...', 12 times, to indicate the significance of Jesus.

> To believe that: Jesus is the Christ the Son of God (6.69; 11.27; 20.31); I am (8.24; 13.19); the Father sent Jesus (11.42; 17.8,21); the Father is in Jesus and Jesus in the Father (10.38; 14.10); Jesus has come from God (16.27,30).

The use of this construction indicates the perception and understanding of authentic faith. This is emphasized in its use with the verbs of knowing (6.69; 10.38; 16.30; 17.8,21, compared with 17.23). There are a number of confessions of faith made by individuals (6.69; 11.27; 16.30). But in each instance what follows shows that faith was not authentic at the time the confession was made (6.70f. (13.36ff.); 11.39; 16.31).

Only 25 uses of 'believe' occur in narrative passages. Here the themes of rejection and partial faith are stated. Confessions of faith are brought into question by their context. All of the constructions are used to indicate partial faith, though 'believe in' is used more frequently in this sense than any other. But the majority of references occur in the discourses where the nature of authentic faith is described.

Four references are noteworthy in that they speak of belief in the future tense (1.7; 17.21; 19.35; 20.31). Witness has the function and purpose of provoking belief. The Gospel affirms the coming of authentic faith and portrays Jesus' ministry in the light of that certainty. Thus descriptions of those who came to partial faith during Jesus' ministry are used as examples of the possibility of coming to authentic faith. There is no difference in terminology between the partial faith described in the narratives and authentic faith described in the discourses. During Jesus' ministry the words and events could only provoke partial faith. From the perspective of the Gospel the same words and events have become the witness which may lead men to authentic faith (20.31).

The use of the verb 'to believe' concentrates attention on Christ. In the Gospel, the reader is called on to believe in Jesus, his Word, his works, and certain facts relating to his relationship with the Father. But these are not ultimate distinctions. Jesus' words are self-testimony. To believe him is to believe in him. He is the content of his own message and because of this, John has designated him the Logos.

The place of believing is further emphasized by the fact that all major and most minor characters affirm or deny faith in Jesus in the course of the Gospel:

1. The disciples, as individuals (1.50; 6.69; 20.8,29), or as a group, (2.11,22; 16.27,30; 17.18), are described as believers more frequently than anyone else. But there are indications that, in the context of Jesus' ministry, even they did not truly believe (2.22; 16.31).

2. After the disciples, 'the many' are most frequently described as believers. This belief is normally in response to signs (2.23; 7.31; 8.30; 10.42; 11.45; 12.11). Such faith is called into question (2.23ff.). In 8.30, 'the many' are identified with the Jews of 8.31. They, more frequently than any, are those of whom it is said, they do not believe (5.38–47; 8.45–46; 9.18; 10.25,26; 12.37).

With the theme of believing, we are faced with the problem of the merging of two perspectives, that of Jesus' ministry and that of the post-resurrection situation. But John's understanding of faith depends on the validity of that distinction. Consequently we now turn to the varying responses of faith, based on signs (2.23ff., etc.); the witness of Jesus' works (10.37f., 14.10f.); Jesus' Word (5.31; 8.18); and the apostolic witness (15.26f., 17.20ff.).

Superficial Faith

Superficial faith was expressed during the time of Jesus' ministry. Such faith indicates the attraction of people to Jesus as a miracle worker, teacher, prophet, or even the Messiah. The form of the statement in 2.23 reveals certain characteristics of the popular, superficial faith.

(*a*) The words 'many believed' are used (2.23; 4.39,41; (6.2), 7.31; 8.30; 10.42; 11.45,48; 12.11,42).

(*b*) The aorist tense is normally used, drawing attention to the specific situation without indicating whether such faith will grow or disappear. The contexts show that this faith had yet to face the scandal of Jesus' claims about himself, and in many cases it proved to be transitory. But there were those who went on to believe authentically.

(*c*) This faith arose out of seeing Jesus' signs (2.23ff.; 3.2; 6.2,14ff.; 7.31; 9.16; 10.41–42; 11.45,47f.; 12.18,19,37,42). While this was a real turning to Jesus, it is shown to be inadequate (2.24) because such believers wanted to find the fulfilment of their own purpose in him (6.15; 12.13ff.).

(*d*) Misunderstanding marks this faith. The misunderstandings are characteristic of the Jewish situation. Jesus confronted those who understood him in Jewish categories, especially the category of the political Messiah, with the scandal of his self-testimony. Thus the existence of misunderstanding reminds us of the historical perspective, and it is used by John as a motif to clarify the understanding of the person of Christ for the reader. The problem was not merely that the Jews did not know that Jesus was the Messiah, nor that they misunderstood the role in terms of a conquering king rather than suffering service. John emphasizes that Jesus is the one in whom God is present and active in his love for the world.

The misunderstanding motif is historically based, dramatically developed and has a pedagogical purpose in the structure of the Gospel. John wrote to remove inadequate attitudes to Jesus which would not be able to stand the test of Jewish persecution. His aim was to provoke faith in Jesus as the incarnate Word, faith which perceives Jesus' unique place in salvation history (20.31). In the Gospel, misunderstanding is confronted with Jesus' self-testimony, which scandalized the crowds and produced murmurings (6.41,43,61; 7.38; cf. 1 Cor. 10.10; Exod. 16.2; Num. 14.2,36; 17.6–15). The murmurings indicate the dissatisfaction of the believers in the one who had not measured up to their expectations. Jesus had no intention of fulfilling their expectations, and confronted them with his claim (6.26ff.). This led to division (7.43; 9.16; 10.19 and also 3.19–21,36; 7.31,40–44,45–52; 8.30ff.; 9.16,39–41; 10.19–21,31–32; 11.45; 12.37–43), the rejection of faith by some of those who had originally believed (6.64–66), and the affirmation of faith by 'the twelve' through Peter (6.68ff.; cf. Mark 9.27ff.).

Authentic Faith

Authentic faith is expressed in the terms of a number of confessions in the Gospel (1.14,49f.; 2.11; 4.42,53; 6.68–69; 9.35–38; 11.27; 16.29–30). But superficial faith cannot be distinguished from authentic faith by the formula used.

Chapter 1 verse 14 does not fit into the historical context of Jesus' ministry. It is a reminiscence ('we beheld' is in the aorist tense, indicating the historical nature of the revelation) placed at the beginning of the Gospel to show the perception of faith. This perception is fundamental to the nature of authentic faith, and is characteristically expressed in the statements using the 'believe that ...' construction which is often linked with verbs of knowing.

But in the historical situation, the faith of individuals like Nathaniel (1.49), though shown to be inadequate (1.51), had a quality which distinguished it from the superficial faith of the crowds. While his faith was inadequate, it expressed his comitment as far as the historical situation would allow. His faith would assuredly develop, and this certainty is expressed in the words, 'You shall see ...', whereas a hypothetical question was put to the crowds, 'What if you see ... ?' (6.62). What distinguishes the faith of Nathaniel from that of the multitude is not greater perception, but the reality of his decision and his willingness to obey Jesus.

The confessions of 4.42 and 4.53 foreshadow the Samaritan and gentile missions, and in 9.35–38 the man who had been blind becomes the example of the true believer in the Jewish situation.

The narrative confessions of faith (6.68f.; 11.27; 16.29–30) are capable of being understood at two levels, and there are sufficient reminders that authentic faith is not yet a reality (6.70–71; 11.39; 13.2,38; 16.31–32). The expressions foreshadow the development of the fullness of faith. They are assessments in retrospect which recognize an integrity lacking in the faith of the multitudes. Faulty perception led to the defection of the disciples. But the integrity of their faith led to reinstatement.

The historical perspective is not rejected by the use of confessions of faith in the Gospel, because John systematically develops the reasons why authentic faith could come only after the time of Jesus' ministry. He had pedagogical reasons for placing the confessions in the context of Jesus' ministry. The words and works of Jesus could not provoke authentic faith during his ministry, but the reminiscence of them in the apostolic witness could. What brought about this change of situation?

1. The glorification or uplifting of the Son of Man (3.14; 8.28; 12.23,31f.; 13.31) revealed the glory of God in his love for the world. This event was crucial for the perception and understanding of authentic faith. It also brought about the effective judgement of the world by which Jesus overcame the blinding work of the power of darkness, making the perception of faith possible.

2. Great stress is laid on belief in the risen Lord (20.8,18,20,25, 27–29). Through the resurrection, the disciples became aware of the true significance of Jesus.

3. The coming of the Paraclete is associated with Jesus' glorification (7.37ff.; 16.7ff.). The Paraclete also brings about the judgement of the world. Judgement began with the coming of Jesus, reached a critical stage at his glorification, and continues to be made effective by the Paraclete until it is finally accomplished by the Son of Man. But, in relation to the believing eye-witnesses, the Paraclete brought about remembrance of Jesus' words (14.26). The perspective of remembrance is that of Jesus' resurrection, his glorification (2.22; 12.16). The context in which Jesus is understood is the salvation history of the Old Testament. Thus the events remembered are unchanged,

but the memory was transformed by a new perspective (Jesus' glorification), a new context (the Old Testament), and a new inspiration (the Paraclete).

Believing is an eschatological phenomenon because it is a response to the eschatological event. It involves a perception that was possible only after the glorification of Jesus. It is a gift of the eschatological age, made possible by the coming of Jesus, but made actual by the coming of the Paraclete.

The *decision* involved in believing is set against the background of Jewish persecution. The necessity of this decision is only clear when it is recognized that the eschatological revelation surpassed all previous revelations. It is the decision to follow Jesus no matter what the cost. The reality of the decision is worked out in obedience to Jesus' word, in the willingness to confess him openly no matter what the cost, and in loving service after the pattern of Jesus' own love (13.35). Both of these aspects of obedience are to be understood as the eschatological gifts of the Spirit to believers.

Faith is the eschatological gift to those who respond with integrity to the revelation in Jesus, whose coming potentially broke the grip of the power of darkness over men. To those who take advantage of the opportunity created by his coming, the Paraclete brings the gift of authentic faith.

All men are the creation of the Word. Response to the Word is a possibility given in creation. The problem concerns the origin of the rejection of the Word by men. John explains this in terms of the power of darkness, the prince of this world, who has perverted and blinded man. The coming of the incarnate Word in judgement broke the grip of the power of darkness, so that men could leave the darkness for the light which had confronted them in Jesus. Those who came to him were given the Paraclete, through whom authentic perception, decision, and obedience became actual in the world. This is a phenomenon of the eschatological age of salvation.

8 *The Response to the Revelation II—Knowledge, Witness and Love*

THE PLACE OF KNOWLEDGE

The nouns 'knowledge' and 'faith' are never used in John, but the verbs 'know' and 'believe' are used frequently.

	JOHN 1–12	JOHN 13–21	TOTAL	PAUL	SYNOPTICS	1 JOHN	N.T. TOTAL
knowledge (*gnōsis*)	0	0	0	23	2	0	29
to know (*ginōskein*)	33	23	56	49	61	25	221
to know (*eidenai*)	54	31	85	102	72	15	230

John's preference for the verb 'to know', rather than the noun 'knowledge', is consistent with the overwhelming pattern in the New Testament. John also has a preference for the verb 'believe' rather than the noun 'faith'. Looked at from this point of view, it is absurd to suggest that John's failure to use 'knowledge' is an anti-Gnostic technique. But with Wisdom and apocalyptic writings, John shares the growing emphasis on knowledge and the tendency towards dualistic thought.

Two other aspects of John's use of knowledge draw attention to the Old Testament background.

(*a*) The two verbs translated 'know' are used as equivalents as they are in the Septuagint, the Greek version of the Old Testament. John's preference for *eidenai* occurs in narrative passages. The two verbs are used almost the same number of times in discourse passages, thirty-five or thirty-six times each.

(*b*) Knowing and believing are inseparable. In the Qumran *War Scroll* the expression is used, 'to know him (God) by faith . . .' (1 QM 13.2–3 and 1 QH 16.14–18).

In the Old Testament and in the Qumran texts, God's know-

> ledge of man implied more than awareness of him. It involved God's choice of and presence with him. Man's knowledge of God involved obedience. The nations did not know God, but Israel should have known him, and the failure to know him brought judgement. Out of judgement grew the hope of a restored Israel and a universal knowledge of God. While a mutual relationship between God and his people is presupposed, there is no statement in the Old Testament in terms of the 'mutual knowledge' expressed in John 10.14–15. But it was from the Old Testament background, where knowledge, faith and love were closely related, that John developed his understanding of knowledge. What transformed his use of knowledge was his understanding of the place of Christ as the revelation of God.

John differs from the Old Testament, which looks to the future for the coming of the knowledge of God, because of his understanding of the person of Christ. The knowledge of God became a reality with the incarnation of the Word. But the future perspective is not altogether absent (7.17; 8.28,32; 10.38; 13.7,35; 14.20,31; 17.3,23) because the historical event has to be experienced existentially before knowledge becomes effective.

> The fact that the coming of knowledge in the future is always expressed by *ginōskein* is only of grammatical importance, because this tense cannot be supplied by *eidenai*.

From a glance at the statistics, it would seem as if in John knowing is more important than believing. In fact the reverse is the case. Almost one quarter of the uses of 'know' are of no theological importance, but simply describe the knowledge of matters of fact. The combination of knowing and believing is of fundamental importance, drawing attention to the christological understanding of faith. Of course, it then needs to be said that such an understanding has its implication for living in the world.

Before turning our attention to the statements about the believer's knowledge of God in Christ, we should notice that these statements presuppose comparable statements about Jesus' relationship with the Father.

Jesus' unique relationship with the Father is stated in many ways in the Gospel; by the titles attributed to him; by his self-testimony to his unity, oneness, equality with the Father; by the assertion that, because he is loved in a unique way, he alone sees what the Father does, he alone is empowered to make the Father's will actual in the world. We now come to discuss the unique 'mutual knowledge' between the Father and Son (10.15).

Only in 10.14–15 is the formula of 'mutual knowledge' used. It is used to describe the unique relationship between Jesus and the Father as the basis of the mutual relationship between Jesus and his own. While Jesus' claim to know the Father is frequently made, only here does he do so in the context of his claim that the Father knows him. Only here is the Father subject to the verb 'to know'. The relationship described is that which exists between the Father and his unique Son and is thus an eternal relationship (17.26). Nowhere does the theme of God's knowledge of man appear in its Old Testament form. Jesus, the Son, confronts men as the incarnate Word, and displays the knowledge attributed to God in the Old Testament (1.48; 2.24f.; 6.64; 10.14,27; 13.11; 16.19). Jesus is the basis of man's knowledge of God, because his relationship with men is analogous to the Father's relationship with him.

The Father's knowledge of Jesus is to be understood in terms of the Father's initiative in giving Jesus his mission and the means to perform it (10.18). Jesus' knowledge of the Father is expressed in terms of his hearing the Father's Word and communicating it to the world. His continual obedience to the Father is stressed (4.34). The meaning of knowledge in the relationship is complementary. For the Father, it means that he commissions and empowers Jesus. For Jesus, it means his complete obedience to the Father's will. In this way Jesus is the complete revelation of the Father and yet subject to him (3.35; 5.20–26).

Jesus' consciousness of his unique relationship with the Father sets him apart from all other men. All things were given into his hands, but he performed the Father's will with absolute freedom. Because he was conscious of his relationship with the Father, he mediates the knowledge of God to men (11.42; 13.3). Knowing that he had come from the Father and would return to him (his origin and destination), he understood his purpose in the world. Thus his testimony differs from all other human testimony. (6.61,64; 8.14,18; 13.1,11,18; 16.30; 18.4; 19.28).

Just as the Father's knowledge of Jesus is to be understood in terms of the giving of mission and authority, Jesus' knowledge of 'his own' involves calling them to follow him (election) and giving them eternal life. The response of 'his own' is modelled on his response to the Father. They know him in that they hear and follow. This is the obedience of faith. Their mission is patterned on his (17.18; 20.21).

Notice should be taken of the words 'even as' (*kathōs*), which have the force of the phrase 'in the same way' in 10.15; 17.18; 20.21.

It is only believers, 'his own', who share this relationship of knowledge with Jesus. Because the Jews rejected Jesus, the Gospel states that they do not know God, or the Spirit (1.10,11; 7.28; 8.55; 15.21; 16.3; 14.17). The Jews rejected Jesus because they rejected his claim to have come from the Father and set aside his works, the evidence he gave for the truth of his claim. We have already examined the moral and spiritual causes of this as well as the rationalization of arguments.

Knowledge, when it is related to faith, expresses the perception and understanding of faith. Knowing, like believing, may express a partial recognition of Jesus (3.2; 2.23ff.). On the one hand, knowledge may lead to authentic faith, because recognizing the need of the gift of eternal life opens the way for the asking of authentic faith (4.10; 7.37ff.). But recognition and asking cannot be separated as two distinct acts. In terms of development, authentic faith is said to emerge on the basis of knowledge (4.53), and an element of self-understanding needs to be recognized in this. On the other hand, faith may open the way to authentic knowledge (8.31–32). It is the abiding of faith that brings the knowledge of the truth which sets men free from sin. Knowledge of the need for freedom is presupposed. Because the Jews lacked this knowledge, they rejected Jesus' challenge.

Full knowledge, like authentic faith, was not a reality prior to Jesus' glorification. This is shown from time to time by the disciples' failure to understand Jesus (4.32; 10.6; 12.16; 13.7,17; 14.4–9; 16.18; 20.9,14). The confessions of authentic faith and knowledge are proleptic expressions of the fullness which was realized at a later date. It has been emphasized that confessions such as these are used because the Gospel could provoke a response that was not possible in the days of Jesus' ministry (4.42; 6.69; 16.30).

'Believe' and 'know' may be used as synonyms, as in 17.21,25. When used in this way, both words indicate the perceptive element of faith. Both words are capable of covering the full range of perception, or lack of it, from the rejection of the revelation in Jesus, through the recognition of superficial faith, to the full perception of authentic faith.

When used in the sense of the proper response to the revelation, both believing and knowing are the way to receive the gift of eternal life (3.15ff.; 17.3). It is no more true to say that knowledge is eternal life (as Bultmann does) than to say believing is eternal life. Eternal life includes authentic faith (knowledge), but also encompasses love, witness, joy and the life of the believer for eternity. Of course, knowledge will involve an awareness of this new situation, and because of this, it is a new self-understanding.

The possibility of knowing God in Jesus continues in the world because Jesus' mission (in its continuing form) was passed on to his disciples (17.20ff.; 20.21f.). Being kept by the power of Jesus' word and the power of the Spirit, their witness and love created the possibility for the world to come to know God in Jesus and receive eternal life. The Gospel is the record of such witness (20.31; 21.24).

KNOWLEDGE EXPRESSED IN WITNESS

John's use of the terminology of witness can be compared with that of the Old Testament (John 8.17 and Deut. 17.6), as well as with Greek usage. The evangelist had a trial setting in mind (such as in Jer. 29.23; Isa. 43.10,12; 44.8; 55.4). The trial portrayed is two-sided. The world had Jesus on trial, but was unable to produce a valid witness. Jesus' witnesses not only cleared him of all charges: their evidence brought the world under judgement.

A look at some statistics will indicate the unique role of the theme of witness in John.

	JOHN 1–12	JOHN 13–21	JOHN TOTAL	PAUL	SYNOPTICS	1 JOHN	N.T. TOTAL
Witness	12	2	14	2	4	6	37
To bear witness	26	7	33	8	2	6	76

The majority of these references have a bearing on the theme of witness borne to Jesus in chapters 1—12. John records the tenfold witness to Jesus, and the Gospel is itself a book of witness. In the context of Jesus' ministry, the most important witnesses were the witness borne by the Father in Jesus' works and Jesus' self-testimony. The function of the other witnesses was to challenge men to take these two witnesses seriously. Ultimately, even the witness of Jesus' works is understood as a challenge to those who were sceptical of Jesus' claims (10.38; 14.11). All of the witnesses have the function of concentrating attention on Jesus' self-testimony. There is no way of avoiding the scandal of his claims by paying attention to other witnesses.

The witness of believers has an added function within the structure and purpose of the Gospel. Time and again John shows that the eye-witness testimony is capable of provoking belief in Jesus (1.7; 4.39; 12.17f.). Faith on the basis of the witness of the first disciples is stated as an assured reality (17.20ff.). This presupposes the inspired testimony of those who had been with Jesus from the beginning (15.26–27). Their testimony was to convict the world of sin, righteousness and judgement (16.8–11).

John emphasizes the unique role of the apostolic testimony for the continuing possibility of faith. The historical nature of that witness is emphasized (15.27; 19.35; 21.24). There is nothing to suggest that the terminology of witness is used loosely. On the contrary, everything suggests that it is used technically of the evidence and the giving of it by first-hand eye-witnesses. John 21.24 claims that the Gospel is the evidence of a first-hand eye-witness. The Gospel is apostolic witness to Jesus after the pattern of 15.26–27. The faith of believers down through the ages is dependent on their testimony (17.20ff.).

KNOWLEDGE EXPRESSED THROUGH LOVE

While the place of love is important in the Gospel, it is faith that is emphasized. But this is reversed in 1 John, which has almost as many uses of love terminology as the Gospel.

	JOHN 1–12	JOHN 13–21	JOHN TOTAL	PAUL	SYNOPTICS	1 JOHN	N.T. TOTAL
love	1	6	7	76	2	18	118
to love (*agapan*)	7	30	37	33	26	27	142
to love (*philein*)	4	9	13	2	8	0	25

John uses the two verbs 'to love' in the same way. This is consistent with the Greek Old Testament, which uses both Greek verbs to translate the same Hebrew word. The fact that John does not use *agapan* of distinctive Christian love and *philein* of something less is shown by the following:

(*a*) Love of the wrong things is expressed using *agapan* (3.19; 12.43).
(*b*) Love in the sense of choice is also expressed using *philein* (12.25; 15.19). The Semitic background is evident in the love-hate contrast.
(*c*) The Father's love for the Son is expressed using both verbs (3.35; 5.20).
(*d*) Even in chapter 21 there is no distinction between the two verbs (21.15–17). While Jesus' question is expressed using *agapan* on the first two occasions, at the third time of asking, and in each of Peter's responses, *philein* is used. But this is not a concession to Peter's weakness because:
   (i) In 21.17, the Gospel reports that Jesus said to Peter the third time. But this is the first time that *philein* is used in the question.
   (ii) If Jesus was speaking Aramaic, such a distinction would have been difficult.
   (iii) The proof of Peter's love is expressed in a way that shows we do not have two different loves.

The emphasis is on the verbal form, 'loving', rather than the abstract notion of love, so that, even when the noun is used, the active sense is carried over into the understanding of it.

John's understanding of love is developed on the basis of the Old Testament and primitive Christian understanding. In the Old Testament, God's love for Israel is primary and the basis of Israel's love for God. Israelites were to show loving-kindness to each other and, where this was absent, it was concluded that Israel did not know God (Deut. 6.44ff.; 7.8; Hosea 2.19; 3.1; 4.1f.; 11.1ff.). Israel's response to God's love is summed up in the Law, and by New Testament times this was summarized in two points (Mark 2.28–33):

(*a*) Love God completely,
(*b*) Love your neighbour as yourself.

John developed the Old Testament understanding in a number of directions. He asserts God's love for the world, not just for Israel (3.16). The universal love of God was not normally acknowledged by the Jews of this period (7.49; 8.48). This is confirmed by the writings of the Qumran Sect (1 QS 1.3ff.).

The New Testament also interprets the command to love the neighbour in universal terms (Luke 10.25–27). Love breaks through the boundaries of legalism and asserts the priority of God's love for the whole world and the possibility that all men may be saved. Where the focus of God's love had been the Exodus event (Hosea 11.1), in John the focus is on the crucified Son, who died that the world might be saved (3.16; 1 John 4.7–11). The changed scope and focus of love in John has produced a distinctive understanding. God's love for the world initiates his saving action. This theme reaches its climax in 1 John 4.8, 'God is love'. Love is safeguarded from misunderstanding by the definitive demonstration in Jesus' act of self-giving. That act of self-giving is not properly understood until faith perceives that it is the act of the Son of God, who has willingly come into the world that the world might be saved. In this regard, faith is the pre-condition of knowledge. Only those who believe can know the love of God revealed in Jesus.

With the definitive demonstration in mind, it is hard to accept the view, put forward by some commentators, to the effect that 'love one another' (13.34f.; 15.12,17) means 'love only believers' (e.g. Käsemann). Support for this view is claimed on the basis that such an attitude existed at Qumran (1 QS 1.3ff., etc.). But the Qumran sect did not have John's understanding of God (3.16). The argument that we should not allow this to affect our understanding of the command to love overlooks the unity of the Gospel. Nor will the argument stand against the evidence in chapters 13—17 because:

(*a*) One purpose of love for the brethren is to make the world recognize Jesus' disciples (13.35). The world is not overlooked.

(*b*) It is not said that believers are to love one another and to hate the unbelievers (this would be the parallel to the expressions at Qumran).

(*c*) The love of God, which he has for Jesus (17.23,26), and for the world (3.16) is to be active in Jesus' disciples (17.26). This implies their love for unbelievers as well as one another.

(*d*) The Father's love for Jesus (15.9) is the basis of his love for his disciples (15.12), which is in turn the basis of the disciples' love for each other. Because of this, their mutual love for each other reveals Jesus' relationship with the Father to the world. Emphasis falls on this aspect because John is concerned with the continuing effect of the revelation in chapters 13—17 (13.35). In this way, the condescending love of God becomes clear. While 'condescending' has become a 'dirty' word, it is difficult to find another which expresses the way that God, in his majesty, reaches down to this benighted world in order that he might raise it up to be with him.

Love needs to be safeguarded from misunderstanding because the world has perverted the love which it knows. The world's love for its own is exclusivist. It hates those who do not belong to it (15.19). The perversion of love (3.19; 12.25,43) through misdirection is an important aspect, explaining the rejection of the love of God in Jesus. Perverted love is conclusive evidence of the absence of the authentic love of the Father (1 John 2.15).

The love of God is to be understood actively, as God graciously reaching out to the world. This love is not to be thought of as having begun at some time. God's love is eternal. It presupposes the eternal love of the Father for the Son (17.24), expressed by the Father:

giving all authority to the Son (3.35);
and showing the Son all that he does (5.20).

The Father's love for the Son meets the response of the Son's love for the Father (14.31; 15.9–10). The Son's love is expressed by obedience to the Father's will. He speaks the Father's words and does only what he sees the Father doing. Thus Jesus is the revelation of the Father, so that to reject him is to reject the Father (10.17; 15.10). Jesus' dignity is expressed in that his relationship with the Father is the basis of the human possibility of being loved by God. It is also shown by the mutual love. It is not only the Father's love for him, but also his love for the Father. Without the response, the possibility bound up with the Father's love remains unfulfilled.

The unfulfilled possibility is expressed when it is said that God loved the world (3.16). While a specific act of love is in view, the continuing attitude of love for the world is presupposed. This love does not have its intended effect because of the world's failure to know God. Thus it is not said that the Father loves the world 'in the same way' (*kathōs*) as he loves the Son, that is, effectively. Because the world rejects God's love, his love can only indicate the possibility which is open to the world. It is possible for the world to come to believe and know and thus to experience eternal life (17.21–26). The existence of those who believe in Jesus is oriented towards bringing the world to believe and know that Jesus has been sent by the Father as his act of love for the world. God's love for the world continues to create the possibility of eternal life for the world.

That we are not talking about a possibility but an actuality in the Father's love for believers is shown by the fact that he loved them 'in the same way' (*kathōs*) as he loved the Son (17.23). Jesus' revealing work was effective because they believed and came to know him as the revelation of the Father. Because of this, the Father's love is in them (17.26). They know that they are loved by the Father, and the character of his love has become real in their lives. This is another way of saying that the believers have eternal life from the Father. The world is loved by God (3.16), but those who do not believe do not have the love of God in them (5.42), they do not have eternal life (6.53; 5.26). Believers have life (3.15f.) and the love of the Father is in them. Through Jesus' Word and the presence of the Spirit, the believers receive the gift of life which is manifest in love.

The meaning of 5.42 is not 'love for God', which could have been expressed quite unambiguously 'you do not love God'. The meaning is rather that those who reject Jesus do not live in the awareness of God's love for them, and consequently they fail to love one another.

One of the great themes of the Gospel is Jesus' love for his disciples. In terms of love, it is matched only by the stress on the need for the disciples to love one another. It is Jesus' love that is emphasized rather than the Father's, because the Father's love is expressed in Jesus. The Father's love is active in him.

Among Jesus' disciples, certain individuals are singled out because of Jesus' special affection for them, Lazarus and Martha (11.3,5), and 'the disciple whom Jesus loved' (13.23; 19.26; 20.2; 21.7,20). But we are more concerned with Jesus' love for his own disciples as a whole, his love for all believers. Jesus' love for his disciples was complete (13.1). Nothing was held back, he gave his life for them (15.13). In another sense, he gave his life for the world (3.16). But the giving only has its life-giving function (intended for all) in those who believe. The world, through unbelief, failed to benefit from the act of love.

Jesus' self-giving can be described as an act of the Father's love (3.16), or an act of Jesus' love (13.1), because Jesus is the revelation of the Father. The divine example of Jesus was to hold good for his disciples. He commanded them to love one another as he had loved them (13.34). He exhorted them to abide in his love (15.9–10,12). Being aware of his love for them, they were to love one another as he loved them. As they are being loved by the Father through the Son, the power of Jesus' life is made effective in them (14.21). They have eternal life and that life has the character of love.

John never speaks of the disciples' love 'for' God, and when he does speak of their love for Jesus, he shows that what he means is in fact believing obedience (the obedience of faith). The Jews who do not believe in Jesus do not love him (8.42). The disciples, who believe, who love Jesus, are to keep his commandments (14.15), to believe in him and to love one another (14.1; 13.34; cf. 1 John 3.23). The response to Jesus' love is faith and love for the brethren. Love for Jesus is understood as obedience (14.23,24). Loving him (believing) in this way enables the disciples to rejoice at his return to the Father (his departure).

> 21.15–17 gives a clear example of the way the disciples' love for Jesus is to be understood. Jesus emphasized, three times, that Peter's love for him was to be expressed in caring for Jesus' flock (sheep or lambs). Previously, Peter had thought that his devotion could be shown by giving his life to save Jesus (13.37). This was to misunderstand Jesus, to think of him simply as another man and not as 'the saviour of the world'. Love for Jesus is to be expressed in the obedience of faith.

The command for the disciples to love one another is emphatic (13.34; 15.12,17). The command is linked with the reminder of Jesus' love because it can only be fulfilled as the disciples are aware of Jesus' love for them. It can only be fulfilled through faith. The example of Jesus' love is repeated in the analogy of 15.13; in the washing of the disciples' feet (13.14ff.) and supremely in laying down his life for them, reminding the reader of the nature of the love by which Jesus' disciples would be known.

Love for one another is only possible for those who abide in Jesus (15.4–17). To abide in Jesus is to abide in his Word (8.32), to keep Jesus' commandment, to abide in Jesus' love. Abiding emphasizes the obedience of faith, through which the believer is aware of Jesus' love, and Jesus' love becomes effective through the believer. Thus it is through Jesus' Word, given to the disciples, and existentially understood in the experience of the Spirit, that the disciples are made one 'in the same way' as the Father and Son are one (17.21ff.).

> The allegory of the vine (15.4–17) has a similar function to Paul's allegory concerning the olive tree (Romans 11.16–21). In both, the branches are broken (cut) off because of unbelief. In John this is expressed in terms of the failure to abide. But

there are two differences which mark John's Jewish (and Paul's gentile) situation. For John Jesus is the vine, the branches are the Jewish believers. This is characteristic of John's christological concentration. In Romans the people of God are the olive tree. Israel is represented by the branches broken off. Israel is no longer the people of God because of unbelief. The branches grafted in are the believing gentiles.

The unity of the Father and Son is a unity of love. The love of the Father is present and active in the Son who comes from the Father to do the Father's will. Jesus' oneness with the Father is expressed in his obedience, and his obedience involves his self-giving to bring life to the world. Jesus' prayer (17.21ff.) was that the disciples might also express this oneness, this unity of love (17.26). As Jesus was sent by the Father, as an expression of his unity with the Father, so 'in the same way' (*kathōs*) Jesus sent his disciples (17.18; 20.21). The unity of the disciples with each other is not directly in view. It is their unity with the Father through the Son (17.21ff.). The disciples' unity and mission are both based on Jesus' unity with and mission from the Father, 'in the same way' (17.21ff.; 17.18; 20.21). The unity is expressed in the descent of love from the Father through the Son to the believers, and through them to the world. Because the love which comes from the Father confronts the world in the life of the believers, the world has its chance to experience that love and believe.

The believer's response of love is described in such a way that no anonymous belief is possible. The believer's manner of life, as much as his confession of faith, is to proclaim the saving love of God in Jesus. Belief in itself involves the believer in God's mission to the world. To believe is to confront the hostile world with God's love, with no other defence than the experience of God's love in Jesus through the power of the Spirit.

LOVE, FAITH AND KNOWLEDGE

John speaks of love in reciprocal terms. But he emphasizes the Father's love for the Son, the Son's love for his disciples, and the disciples' love for one another. Love is understood as the self-giving which is characteristic of God. The movement of God's love, from the Father through the Son to the disciples, has the world in view. God loved the world and gave his Son. But the world has rejected the love of the Father in the Son. The Father's love for the world is not without effect. It is his love which creates the opportunity for the world to respond to his love (3.16; 17.21–26). Love is the action of God, in condescension and humility, for the world, creating the possibility of a relationship with him. Love is expressed through the Son to believers, and through believers to the world. To experience the love of God in Christ is to be caught up into God's mission, because to receive God's loving gift of life is to become a part of the manifestation of God's love for the world.

Love has another meaning where the love of Jesus for the Father and the love of the disciples for Jesus is mentioned. Here the basic meaning is obedience. In the case of the disciples it also carries the qualification that it is the obedience of faith.

> Love for Jesus is understood by the disciples, in the context of Jesus' ministry, as doing something personally for Jesus. Peter offered to give his life to save Jesus. Jesus re-interpreted the claim to love him in terms of believing in him, and obeying his command to love, that is serve the brethren.

Jesus' relationship with the Father is never described as faith. Faith is the response evoked by the revelation of God in Jesus. At the time of Jesus' ministry, faith was dependent on some knowledge of him. It indicated the perception of some significance in him. For those who made a commitment of obedience to Jesus, this beginning of faith came to fulfilment in the post-resurrection authentic faith. This faith is distinguished from superficial faith by the recognition of Jesus' unique person and work in bringing eternal life to men. This knowledge in faith is expressed in obedience.

The Father's knowledge of the Son, like the Son's knowledge of the believers, is expressed in terms of the giving of life and mission. This knowledge is a commissioning. The Son's knowledge of the Father, like the believers' knowledge of the Son, is expressed in obedience. But where Jesus' knowledge of the Father is direct, the disciples' knowledge of Jesus is qualified by believing. It is not a direct knowledge. This is true even of the first disciples, because their knowledge of the significance of Jesus only dawned after he had departed and the Spirit had come.

Knowledge, like love, is used to describe the relationships between the Father and the Son, and the Son and his disciples. Unlike love, knowledge is never used to express the unfulfilled possibility for the world—God loved the world. Love makes a relationship with God possible for the world. Where love and knowledge are mutual, they describe similar activities. Where God's love for the world is rejected there is no mutual knowledge, and knowledge is an inappropriate description. Love indicates the possibility of which mutual knowledge should be the fulfilment. God's love can only be known through believing in Jesus, in knowing him and being known by him. God loved the world, but it is not said that he knows it. This would be to make actual what love had made possible, that is, eternal life. But the world rejected the knowledge of God in Jesus (1.10–11).

The terms knowledge and love are used to show that the disciples' relationship with Jesus is on the pattern (*kathōs*) of his relationship with the Father (10.14–15; 15.10; 17.23; 20.21). 'Mutual' or 'reciprocal' love (and knowledge) does not mean that the love (and knowledge) on both sides is identical. On the contrary, the relationship is complementary. The Father's love and knowledge of Jesus, and Jesus' love and knowledge of believers, are expressed in giving life and mission. Jesus' knowledge of the Father involves his obedience to and ability to make the Father known. The believer's knowledge of Jesus is the perception of Jesus as the revelation of the Father which issues in obedience to his word of love. Thus the believer is caught up into God's mission of love to the world, that the world may come to know and believe in Jesus as the revelation of the Father's love for the world.

While the emphasis is on believing in John 1–12, love becomes central in John 13–17. But there it is love as the basis of the possibility that the world might come to believe. Thus the focus remains on faith. In 1 John the focus is on love as a test of all claims to know God.

PART THREE

Interpreting 1 John

1 1 John and the Fourth Gospel

The questions concerning the relation of 1 John to the Fourth Gospel and the background of 1 John are closely related. The thought and language of both books are sufficiently similar to raise the question of common authorship and background. Differences occur, but the means by which these are to be explained as yet has received no conclusive answer. In fact there is no unanimous recognition of what the differences actually are. C. H. Dodd argues that the stylistic and theological differences are sufficient to indicate two different authors. W. F. Howard drew attention to the marked stylistic similarities between the two books. Rudolf Bultmann thinks that a common source was used by the authors of 1 John and the Gospel, thus indicating his view of the stylistic similarities. The argument on the basis of style would seem to have reached an impasse.

Bultmann proposes a source and redaction theory for the composition of 1 John similar to his well-known theory concerning the composition of the Gospel, and the theory is no more acceptable with regard to 1 John. Nor does the source theory propounded by Dr J. C. O'Neill seem likely to win many supporters. He has argued that the basis of 1 John is to be found in 'twelve poetic admonitions' originally belonging to the writings of a Jewish sect similar to that of Qumran, and has drawn attention to the fact that the thought, language and style of 1 John have parallels to the Qumran texts in some respects. This is something that has been the focus of attention with regard to the Fourth Gospel, and would seem to point in the direction of the affirmation of common authorship and background of the Fourth Gospel and 1 John. But the suggestion that the opponents of 1 John were Jews who failed to accept Jesus as the Messiah seems to raise an insurmountable objection to this theory. If the author of 1 John did use sources, neither Bultmann nor O'Neill has succeeded in isolating and identifying them. Their arguments do suggest that the stylistic evidence cannot bear the weight of the theory of separate authorship.

C. H. Dodd has argued that the Epistle can be distinguished from the Gospel by its closer relation to primitive Christianity and Gnosticism.

1. *1 John and Gnosticism*. Dodd considers that the Epistle is more naïvely open to Gnosticism than the Gospel. Gnostic language is certainly more apparent in the Epistle, although the Epistle shares certain Gnostic expressions with the Gospel, such as 'life-giving knowledge', 'knowledge of the truth which liberates', 'regeneration', 'vision of God', 'union with God', and also the dualistic tendency to divide mankind into two classes. On the last point Dodd claims that the Epistle is less guarded and closer to Gnosticism than the Gospel. This is also indicated in the statements 'God is light', 'God is love', the divine 'seed' (*sperma*), 'chrism' (*chrisma*), and in the argument implied in the statement, 'We know that if he is manifested we shall be like him, because we shall see him as he is.'

Contrary to Dodd, the Epistle is more consciously anti-Gnostic than the Gospel. In the Gospel terms are used without explanation which could only be used in the Epistle with careful clarification. Where the evangelist was concerned to emphasize that Jesus was truly divine (in the context of the Jewish rejection of the revelation of Jesus), 1 John was written to assert that Jesus Christ was truly man (in the context of the Gnostic rejection of his humanity). By the second century the Gospel was misunderstood in Gnostic terms by Gnostic commentators, but 1 John was written to defend the Johannine language against Gnostic misunderstanding.

Dodd interprets knowledge of and union with God in terms of Gnostic mystical vision. But in the Gospel and Epistle this is modified in two ways. Firstly, to see Jesus is to see God. Secondly, 'we have seen' is the affirmation of all who share in the apostolic witness through faith. To believe is to see God. But on this matter Dodd has expressed two different views. In his commentary on *The Johannine Epistles* and his *Historical Tradition in the Fourth Gospel*, Dodd interprets 'we have seen' in terms of the awareness of 'corporate personality' (community solidarity) in the Old Testament, but in *The Interpretation of the Fourth Gospel* he suggests that Hellenistic mysticism is the background to the Johannine interpretation of faith as vision.

Neither of these interpretations does justice to the claim

of the Gospel and Epistle to embody apostolic eye-witness testimony (John 1.14; 19.35; 21.24; and especially 1 John 1.1ff.). In the Gospel, seeing Jesus is certainly not equated with believing nor is believing seeing. There are those who have seen and believed and those who themselves have not seen but who have believed on the basis of the word (witness) of those who have seen (John 20.29; 17.20).

Dodd suggests that the Epistle is closer to Gnosticism than the Gospel in its treatment of initiation into knowledge. The idea of regeneration (in the Gospel and Epistle) is said to be derived from Hellenistic mysticism. While the Spirit is the agent of regeneration in the Gospel, the divine 'seed' (*sperma*) effects regeneration in the Epistle, as in Gnosticism. But Dodd admits that the 'seed' is not understood in the Gnostic sense. The 'seed' is the Word of God. In the Epistle, initiation into knowledge is also said to take place through 'anointing' (*chrisma*). This 'anointing' is related to but not to be equated with baptism. The 'seed' is the Word of God and 'anointing' is to be understood as the rule of faith confessed at baptism. Thus Dodd has shown that initiation in 1 John is closer to primitive Christianity than to Gnosticism. The language of regeneration also has a background in Judaism, for example, 'those born of the truth ...' (1 QS 3.19) and the primitive Christian tradition (James 1.18; 1 Peter 1.3,23; Titus 3.5). The added prominence of regeneration in 1 John might be the result of conflict with Gnosticism (1 John 2.29; 3.9; 4.7; 5.1,4,18; but only in John 1.12f.; 3.3–8).

Dodd's contrast between the Spirit (in the Gospel) and the Word (in the Epistle) as the agents of regeneration is not valid because the 'anointing' is from 'the Holy One' (1 John 2.20), which is probably a reference to the Holy Spirit. The Gospel also teaches that faith in Jesus (the Word) is a prerequisite for the new birth by the Spirit (John 1.12f.; 3.14ff.). In the Epistle the relation between the confession of faith in Jesus, the Spirit and baptism constitutes a logical development for the age of the Church.

Greater differences between the Gospel and Epistle can be seen in the statements defining God in terms of being, 'God is light', 'God is love' (1 John 1.5; 4.8). In the Gospel, 'God is Spirit' is only a partial parallel in terms of form (John 4.24, *pneuma ho theos* and see *hoti ho theos phōs estin,* 1 John 1.5; and *hoti ho theos agapē estin,* 1 John 4.8). In terms of content the statements differ because 'God is Spirit' has Old Testament precedent, where God who is Spirit is contrasted with man who is flesh (Isa. 31.3; 40.6–8; Jer. 17.5). But the difference is not great because 'love' and 'light' are understood dynamically. The statements are extensions of the Christology of the Gospel, where Jesus is the light of the world (8.12; 9.5) and the love of God is to be seen in the giving of the Son (3.16) as in the Epistle (1 John 2.2; 4.8f.). In the Epistle, 'light' has taken on an ethical emphasis due to the conflict with Gnosticism. Because the heretics had rejected the apostolic witness to the revelation in Christ, the christological statements of the Gospel are taken back to their theological origin in 1 John.

2. 1 *John and Primitive Christianity*. Dodd argues that the author of 1 John shares with the primitive Church (but not the evangelist) his views on eschatology, the Spirit and the work of Christ.

The author of 1 John gives no expression to the evangelist's interpretation of eschatology in terms of the resurrection and the coming of the Paraclete. For him, eschatology involved the future coming of Christ and the great day of judgement. But Dodd's suggestion that the evangelist absorbs the eschatological emphasis (or reinterprets it in realized terms) overlooks the teaching about the coming of Jesus and judgement on the last day (John 5.21ff.; 6.39,40,44,54; 12.48; 14.3; 17.24). This future eschatological emphasis is noted by most scholars but some, like Bultmann, attribute it to a later redaction. What is more, the element of realization is not absent from the Epistle (2.8; 5.20).

The distinctive teaching of the Gospel about the Spirit is not to be found in the Epistle. In the Gospel the Holy Spirit, the Spirit of Truth, is also named the Paraclete but in the Epistle, although the Spirit is called the Spirit of Truth (and the Holy One), Jesus is described as our advocate (Paraclete) with the Father. In the Epistle (and the primitive Church) the Spirit is primarily the Spirit of prophecy through which the truth of the gospel is confirmed to those who hear. But because there is also false inspiration, inspiration itself cannot be used as a criterion of truth. Confession of the rule of faith is the criterion of true inspiration (1 John 4.2). Dodd also claims that the Epistle teaches that the gift of the Spirit is the interior witness, the immediate, spontaneous, unanalysable awareness of the divine presence which has as its external complement the testimony to Christ in the rule of faith.

But the differences are not as clear as Dodd suggests. Firstly, 'the Spirit of Truth' is referred to as 'another Paraclete' (John

14.16), perhaps implying that Jesus was the original Paraclete. Jesus' advocacy with the Father for us (1 John 2.1) is described in John 17. In the Gospel, the Spirit is the Paraclete of the Father and Son with the believer, while Jesus is the believer's Paraclete with the Father in the Epistle.

Secondly, the Spirit inspires witness in the Gospel (15.26–27) as in the Epistle (4.1ff.). The Spirit is 'the power within the Church which brings forth both knowledge and the proclamation of the Word' (Bultmann). But there is no mention of the possession of the Spirit in terms of subjective experience in 1 John. Of course, the confession of faith is rooted in experience, but it is the confession rather than any pattern of experience that manifests the activity of the Spirit.

Belief that God had revealed himself in Christ was at the heart of the rule of faith. In the crisis faced by 1 John, the truth was expressed in terms of the incarnation, Jesus Christ has come in the flesh. (In the confrontation with Judaism the Gospel stressed that the Word became flesh.) By the test of the teaching of the reality of the incarnation, the teaching of the heretics was condemned, no matter how powerfully inspired.

The primitive Christian rule of faith also included statements about the work of Christ. Dodd thinks that 1 John is closer to this (than the Gospel) in the use of 'expiation' (*hilasmos*) (2.2; 4.10), and the distinctive teaching of the evangelist is overlooked.

While the evangelist does not use the term 'expiation', his interpretation of the work of Christ is consistent with the interpretation in the Epistle. Jesus removed the stain of sin because in his death and resurrection sin 'was, so to speak, neutralized, and its corruption sterilized, by the love and power of God' (Dodd). (Compare 1 John 1.7; 2.2; 4.10; and John 1.29,36; 11.50–52; 13.1–17.) Jesus, as the lamb of God, bears away the sin of the world (John 1.29), he was manifested to take away sin (1 John 3.5).

In both the Gospel and Epistle the work of Christ is described from six different perspectives.

(*a*) Sacrificial terms are used to describe the way sin is neutralized, but no precise interpretation is given. Perhaps 1 John has taken a further step in explanation in using the word 'expiation'.
(*b*) Jesus is described as the saviour of the world (John 3.16; 4.42 and 1 John 4.14).
(*c*) Jesus came to destroy the works of the devil (John 3.19ff.; 5.22; 9.39; 12.31f.; and 1 John 3.8,12; 5.5f.,18f.). The world still

lies in the grip of the evil one, but it is a broken grip for all who believe. Faith is victory (1 John 5.4).

(*d*) Jesus' work is described in terms of revelation (John 1.14–18; 1 John 4.12; 5.20). Ignorance of the true God has been abolished through the revelation in the Son.

(*e*) The revelation is described in terms of the love of God (John 3.16; 1 John 4.8–9). It is this love that brings life to the world and it was revealed in the giving of the Son for the life of the world.

(*f*) Jesus is called the believer's advocate with the Father in 1 John and his advocacy is described in the Gospel (John 17).

The distinctive interpretation of the death and resurrection of Jesus in terms of the release of his life for the world was first made popular by B. F. Westcott in his commentary on the Johannine Epistles. If it is in the Gospel, it would also seem to be in the Epistle. But the evangelist does not equate the return of Jesus with the coming of the Spirit (Jesus' life released for the world). This view fails to take account of the relation between Jesus and the Spirit and the unfulfilled nature of the eschatological hope.

Dodd's analysis of the theological differences between the Gospel and 1 John is unconvincing. The Gospel also expresses what Dodd describes as the primitive Christian views on eschatology, the Spirit, and the work of Christ, though there are a few differences in terminology. The Epistle, while it does use some expressions which may be derived from Gnosticism, is not more open to this heresy than the Gospel. In fact the terminology is more consciously guarded against Gnosticism in the Epistle than the Gospel. This is due to the confrontation with the heresy reflected in the Epistle. Because of this, the emphasis has moved from the acceptance in faith of the divine revelation in Jesus to the historical nature of the revelation with its ethical implications. Because the heretics rejected the historical revelation as witnessed to by the apostles, the argument in 1 John is that those who reject the historical revelation (Christology) reject the knowledge of God (theology). Thus the statements about Christ in the Gospel are taken back to their theological origin in 1 John.

The differences between the Gospel and 1 John are not due to independent authors but to the different situations for which each book was written.

2 *The Structure*

The structure of 1 John, or the lack of it, has been the subject of much discussion. Each passage is clear enough in itself, but there is no clear progression of thought throughout the book.

Robert Law (*The Tests of Life*, 1909, p. 5) drew attention to the 'spiral' development of argument and the Hebraic poetic style, similar to the parallelism of the Wisdom literature. He suggested that the Epistle consists of an introduction followed by three cycles. In the cycles, the claims of the heretics are tested by the standards of (1) righteousness (2) love (3) belief. A summary of Law's analysis follows:

I. Prologue (1.1–4).

II. *First Cycle*: The Christian life as walking in the light (1.5—2.28).
- (a) Introduction (1.5–7).
- (b) Tested by righteousness (1.8—2.6).
- (c) Tested by love (2.7–17).
- (d) Tested by belief (2.18–28).

III. *Second Cycle*: The Christian life as Divine Sonship (2.29—4.6).
- (a) Tested by righteousness (2.29—3.10a).
- (b) Tested by love (3.10b–24a).
- (c) Tested by belief (3.24b—4.6).

IV. *Third Cycle*: Correlation of righteousness, love and belief (4.7—5.21).
1. *Love* (4.7—5.3a).
   - (a) The genesis of love (4.7–12).
   - (b) The synthesis of love and belief (4.13–16).
   - (c) The effect, motives and manifestations of love (4.17—5.3a).
2. *Belief* (5.3b–21).
   - (a) The power, content, basis and issue of Christian belief (5.3b–12).
   - (b) The certainties of Christian belief (5.13–21).

Law's analysis looks reasonable at first sight, but the whole pattern breaks down in the third cycle. A similar analysis was produced by

Theodor Häring, with one significant difference. Häring suggests that there are only two leading tests in each cycle, the ethical test (combining love and righteousness), and the christological test (the test of belief). While Law rejected the identification of righteousness and love, he admitted that Häring's analysis gives a more logical division than his own. A Summary of Häring's analysis can be given as follows:

I. Introduction (1.1–4).

II. *First presentation of the two tests* (1.5—2.27). The two tests of fellowship with God (ethical and christological theses).
   1. Walking in the light the true sign of fellowship with God (ethical test). Refutation of the first lie (1.5—2.17).
   2. Faith in Jesus Christ as the test of fellowship with God (christological thesis). Refutation of the second lie (2.18–27).

III. *Second presentation of the two tests* (2.28—4.6). With special emphasis on their connection (3.22–24).
   1. Doing righteousness (love of the brethren) the sign by which we may know that we are born of God (2.28—3.24).
   2. The christological thesis. The Spirit from God confesses Jesus Christ has come in the flesh (4.1–6).

IV. *Third presentation of the two theses* in which their inseparable relation to each other is shown (4.7—5.12).
   1. Love, based on faith in the revelation of love, is the proof of knowing God and being born of God (4.7–21).
   2. Faith is the foundation of love (5.1–12).

V. *Conclusion* (5.13–21).

Häring's analysis (and Law's), with its emphasis on the tests, highlights the conflict with the heretics and emphasizes that the Epistle was written to confirm the awareness that believers have eternal life (5.13). Häring's conclusion that doing righteousness is in essence identical with love of the brethren is the basis of his twofold test structure. In this he has been followed (in broad terms) by both Brooke and Bultmann. The analysis has its merits, but the pattern tends to be imposed rather than discovered and 'perhaps the attempt to analyse the Epistle should be abandoned as useless' (Brooke, p. xxxii).

Bultmann, having attempted an analysis as far as 2.27, asserts:

'Attempts to find a train of thought in 2.28—5.12 are futile' (Bultmann, p. 43). This section is a compendium of fragments supplementing 1.5—2.27. He postulates that a source (similar to the revelation discourses used in the Gospel) underlies the whole work. But the use of the source varied in the different sections.

> The source underlying 1.5—2.27 consists of 1.6–7a,8,10; 2.4–5, 9–11. The same source underlies 2.28—3.24 but is less extensive, 2.29b; 3.4a,6,7b,8a,9, and is suggested more tentatively in 4.1—5.12, 4.7a,8a,(12?), and underlying 5.1b–2,12.

The original composition was produced as the author commented on his source and 1.1–2.27 was the result. Later additions were made, perhaps by the same author or possibly by his disciples, producing 1.1—5.13. After completion the work was tampered with by an 'ecclesiastical redactor' who added the appendix (5.14–21), traditional emphases concerning the work of Christ and eschatology (1.7b,9b; 2.2,15–17,(28?); (3.2?); 4.10b, 'the day of judgement' 4.17; 5.7–8).

J. C. O'Neill has suggested that the lack of structure can be explained on the basis of a source theory. The composition is based on 'twelve poetic admonitions' which originated in a Jewish sect to which the author had belonged. He and other members of the sect became Christians, and the author enlarged on the admonitions in order to persuade the remainder that Jesus really was the Messiah. Thus 'his opponents were the members of the Jewish sect who had refused to follow their brethren into the Christian movement' (p. 6, *The Puzzle of 1 John*).

The twelve poetic admonitions can be outlined as follows:

1. 1.6–10, less 'the blood of Jesus his Son', 1.7.
2. 2.1a,3–5, (2.1b,2,6 are Christian additions).
3. 2.7,9–11, (2.8 is an addition).
4. 2.14–17b, (2.17c is a pious addition).
5. 2.18,20,21,27, (2.19,22–26 and the last phrase of 2.27 are additions).
6. 2.28–29; 3.1–4,7–8a,9–10, (3.5,6,8b are additions).
7. 3.10b–12a,15,17–19a, (3.12b–14,16 are additions).
8. 3.19b,20b–22,24 (3.20a,23 and the last phrase of 3.24 are additions).
9. 4.1,4–6, (4.2–3 are additions).
10. 4.7–8,12–13,16b–18, (4.9,10,14,15,16a are additions).

11. 4.19–21; 5.1b–4a, (5.1a,4b–13 are additions).
12. 5.14–19,21, (5.13,20 are additions).

The additions noted indicate the Christian comment on the original Jewish sources.

The source theories of Bultmann and O'Neill suffer from two serious problems. (1) The pre-Christian source includes the corrections as well as the false claims (e.g. the antitheses of 1.6,8,10; 2.4,9). What is the point of the corrections if they belong to the heretical source? (2) The source is reconstructed by removing 'Christian additions'. Is it any surprise that what remains is a (non) pre-Christian source? Added to this there is no agreement as to what constitutes the source nor what is the character of the source. O'Neill thinks that the source originated in a Jewish sect and has a style akin to *parallelismus membrorum* of the Old Testament (p. 8). But Bultmann rejects this comparison and claims that the source has the style of the Gnostic revelation discourses (p. 17, n. 10). Bultmann concludes that O'Neill's theory of a Jewish source with Christian comment is unconvincing, but admits that he 'must be credited with showing that 1 John presupposes the Jewish language-tradition and thought-world' (p. 2). But this admission has not changed Bultmann's approach to 1 John. Perhaps the truth lies on both sides. John's opponents were surely Gnostics, and the controversy is to be understood in that context rather than in terms of Messiahship in the context of Judaism. But the language and thought of the author reflect a Jewish background.

Rudolf Schnackenburg, in his great commentary, rightly recognizes the importance of the antitheses, indicating the position of the opponents of the author (p. 1, n. 3). Thus 1 John is, in spite of the lack of formal introductory and concluding greetings, a genuine letter which sets out to oppose the heretical Gnostic enemies of the truth. The double nature of the material is not the result of the author commenting on a source, but is the consequence of the author's double purpose for writing. He wrote to oppose the heretics and to encourage the believers. But 1 John is not a normal letter. Like Hebrews, it can be compared with a tract. But both of these books are addressed to concrete situations and this distinguishes them from tracts in general, and 1 John is to be distinguished from Hebrews which, unlike 1 John, treats its theme systematically. The unsystematic treatment of 1 John certainly distinguishes it from Hebrews. It is my contention that this difference does not so much reflect the minds of the authors as the situations which provoked their responses.

Hebrews was written to expose the danger and folly of drifting away from Christ back into Judaism, but 1 John was written to expose heresy within the Christian community. Even when the community was divided by schism, it remained a conflict between those who claimed to be Christians. What this situation required was a critique, in detail, of the errors of the schismatics, whereas Hebrews presents the contrast between the shadow (Judaism) and the reality (Christ). It is interesting to notice that neither 1 John nor Hebrews emphasizes the resurrection of Jesus. In fact this event is mentioned only in Hebrews 13.20. This is a strange contrast with the literature of the New Testament in general. The complete absence of reference to the resurrection of Jesus in 1 John has to be seen over against the strong emphasis on this event in the Gospel of John. The explanation of this phenomenon helps to throw light on the situation. Because Hebrews takes up the theme of the high priesthood of Christ, there are three necessary emphases. (1) As High Priest, Christ represents humanity and participates in the reality of human existence. Thus he is a High Priest who understands and sympathizes with men in their weakness and temptation. (2) As a High Priest he offers himself as the true sacrifice of which the animal sacrifices of the Old Testament were but shadows. (3) After the sacrifice the High Priest appears within the holy of holies. Jesus entered the heavenly place, of which the holy of holies in the Temple was but a shadow, there to appear before the presence of God. Thus in Hebrews the three points of stress are incarnation, death, and exaltation.

In the Gospel of John, the resurrection of Jesus is the clearest demonstration that Jesus of Nazareth was the incarnate divine Word (the unique Son). The Jews claimed that he was a mere man, a sinner, a blasphemer. But in the resurrection he was shown to be the Son of God.

1 John was not written to show that Jesus of Nazareth was divine (against Judaism), but to affirm his real humanity (against Gnosticism) to be the revelation of the character and saving work of God. In this context the importance of the resurrection falls into the background.

3 The Background

It appears to be axiomatic to assume that the background presupposed by the Gospel and 1 John is identical. This is true of those who believe that both books come from the same hand, such as Sir Edwin Hoskyns, 'In the First Epistle of John, which must be assumed to have come from the same hand as the Gospel, a somewhat stronger light is thrown upon the readers of the epistle, and therefore, presumably, upon the original readers of the Gospel also', and J. A. T. Robinson, 'the milieu they (Gospel and Epistles of John) presuppose is so similar that any theory about the nature of the community for which the Gospel was written which will not fit the evidence of the Epistles is bound to be precarious'. It is also true of those who believe that the books were written by different authors, Rudolf Bultmann and C. H. Dodd.

Bultmann's theory (similar to his source and redaction theory concerning the Gospel) is that the author of the Epistle used Gnostic revelation discourses as his basic source. His work was later subjected to additions and alterations by the ecclesiastical redactor. Thus both books were written to counter Gnosticism. But there is a basic difference of perspective between the two books which Bultmann claims decisively indicates that the two books were not written by the same author. In the Gospel the opponents of the truth (the Jews, who represent the world) are outside the Church, but the opponents of the truth in the Epistle are within the Church itself. This changed situation indicates that the Epistle is from a later period than the Gospel.

Contrary to Bultmann, the changed situation does not indicate that the books were written by different authors, but is the means by which the differences between the two books might be explained in terms of a single author.

The evidence of the contents of the Gospel and the relation of its language to the Qumran texts indicate the Jewish background of the Gospel. Judaism was fragmented, and the pressure of the threat of excommunication was used in an attempt to suppress

Jewish Christians. In facing the threat of excommunication, John stressed the nature of the revelation in Jesus. The nature of the revelation presupposed that the response of faith involved an open confession of faith in Jesus. This open confession could only lead to confrontation and an ultimate break with Judaism which would have opened mission to the gentiles. The Johannine language would have had a strong attraction for intellectual or pseudo-intellectual pagans.

The evidence of 1 John suggests that pagans accepted the 'new teaching' enthusiastically. Perhaps this was because the Judaism out of which the Gospel arose, represented by the Qumran texts, had some linguistic affinity with Gnosticism. But it soon became clear that these 'converts' could use John's language with a completely different meaning from that which he intended. In this new situation John was forced to clarify and define the meaning of his terminology to exclude misunderstandings. This is a major difference between 1 John and the Gospel. In the Gospel there is no indication that John was aware that there were those who used the language that he used but with an entirely different sense. When we turn to 1 John the situation has changed. John has now to defend what he has said and to define his terms. This change indicates a move from a Jewish situation where terminology and symbols were interpreted from the perspective of the shared history recorded in the Old Testament (as at Qumran), to a situation where pagans acknowledged no common history but interpreted terms and symbols from the perspective of subjective religious experience. In doing this, they abandoned the control on the meaning of words and symbols provided by the historical perspective. In this situation John asserted the primacy of the witness to the historical revelation (1 John 1.1ff.; 4.1–16.).

4 *The Heresy*

1 John was written at a time of crisis when the Church (at least the congregation to which this letter was addressed) was threatened by heretics who had cut themselves off from the authority

of the apostolic witness to Jesus (2.19; 4.6). They had seemingly been converted but held beliefs incompatible with the Christian faith. Eventually the fact that they were heretics was revealed through schism (2.19).

> Although 1 John never uses the word church (*ekklēsia*) it presents a profound interpretation of the nature of the believing community. The believers are to be a community called into being by the witness to God's saving action in his Son, and the character of the community is derived from the character of the saving action. It is to be the loving community. It is interesting to note that there is nothing of the later 'Catholic' doctrine of the Church, ministry, and sacraments in 1 John. The Church is (as in the Gospel) 'the community under the Word' (Käsemann). It is true that the Word is embodied in the apostolic witness, but their authority is nothing other than as the bearers of the Word. Given this interpretation, to break from the community is to break from the apostolic witness and thus to be cut off from God's saving act. It should also be recognized that in both the Gospel and 1 John the Spirit plays a conservative role directing the believers back to God's saving act in history. According to the Gospel the task of the Spirit is to remind, and in 1 John the Spirit of Truth is recognized in the confession 'Jesus Christ has come in the flesh'.

Though the heretics had withdrawn, the community was in turmoil and continued to be threatened by the false teaching. The heresy consisted both in what was affirmed and what was denied.

The heretics denied that Jesus was the Christ (2.22f.). In this context 'Christ' does not mean 'Messiah' as it does in the Gospel (John 1.41). The meaning was dictated by the use of the term by the heretics. It is consistent with what Irenaeus says of the teaching of Cerinthus, with whom, he said, the apostle John came into conflict. Cerinthus would not allow the higher power, 'Christ', to be identified with the earthly Jesus. He said that the higher power came upon Jesus at his baptism and left him before his passion. In 1 John the denial that Jesus was the Christ was equivalent to denying that Jesus was the Son of God, or to deny that Jesus Christ had come in the flesh (4.2; 5.6).

Against this aspect of the heresy John declares that Jesus is the Christ (5.1); that he is the Son of God (4.15; 5.5ff.); that he came in the flesh (4.2); not in the water of baptism only, but in water and blood, baptism and death (5.6). To reject this was to reject the Father who sent Jesus (4.15; 5.1).

The affirmations of the heretics are indicated by a stylistic device and they, with the denial and antitheses, provide the author with the basic structure of the letter.

The approach suggested here is not a source theory. It is recognized that the heretics were Gnostics (with Bultmann and others), and that the conflict with the heretics runs throughout the Epistle (with Schnackenburg and others). O'Neill rightly claims that Jewish or Gnostic are not mutually exclusive terms, but that does not prove that the heretics were Jewish Gnostics. His argument concerning the controversy about Christ is inconclusive because the designation is open to Gnostic interpretation as well as the Jewish sense of Messiah. What is more, his argument at this point presupposes only a Jewish background, not necessarily a Jewish Gnostic background at all. Against the Jewish background of the heretics it should be noted that there are no Old Testament quotations in 1 John and only one clear reference to the Old Testament in the statement about Cain (Gen. 4.8; 1 John 3.12). The impression that the letter was written to a non-Jewish situation is confirmed by the concluding words, 'Little children, guard yourselves from idols' (1 John 5.21). The Jewish language and style of the letter (to be recognized in relation to the Qumran texts) is the result of the background of the author, not of the readers or the heretics.

The approach suggested is not a source theory. The author was responsible for the whole composition. But he takes up the points which separate his opponents from him, their affirmations, denials, attitudes and behaviour which he considers to be the antitheses to the truth. These are not taken from a source document, but were repeated by the author in the midst of the controversy. Thus the Epistle is structured as a response to the affirmations, denials, attitudes and behaviour of the heretics. Because they represent an identifiable position (they do seem to have differed amongst themselves on some issues), and the author responds to the full range of his disagreements with them, there is a loose unity of the material in the Epistle. Theodor Häring rightly recognized that the differences focused on the christological confession of faith and the ethical life of love.

There are seven affirmations in all. There is:

a threefold use of 'if we say' (1.6,8,10)
a threefold use of 'he who says' (2.4,6,9)
and a single use of 'if anyone says' (4.20)

The position of the heretics is also to be seen in the conflicts and antitheses of another three groups of sayings where the author sets out his position in opposition to the heretics.

(*a*) 1 John 3.7,8,10,14f.; 4.8
(*b*) 1 John 2.29; 3.4,6,9,10
(*c*) 1 John 5.6,10,12,19

From a stylistic point of view these statements are also distinctive. The first group, listed under (*a*), contains statements which begin 'he who', followed by a participle. The second group (*b*) contains statements introduced by 'everyone who' followed by a participle. Two of the statements listed under (*c*) are also introduced by 'he who', but in 5.6 only the author's view is expressed in this form. The antithesis is also expressed without the form in 5.19.

In the first two groups of references, (*a*) and (*b*), the author stresses the active nature of righteousness interpreted in terms of love for the brother. It is love in action not only in word. It excludes sinful action which is interpreted as hatred of the brother.

The third group of references, (*c*), concentrates attention on the witness of the Spirit expressed in the apostolic confession of faith, 'Jesus Christ has come in the flesh'. His coming has drawn out those who no longer belong to the world but to him. They also, as he did, stand in opposition to the world.

In these references the seven affirmations of the heretics are focused on two issues: (1) the confession of faith in Jesus Christ come in the flesh, and (2) the necessity of a life of active love for the brother. Both points were rejected by the heretics, who affirmed a direct mystical knowledge of God, bypassing the witness to the revelation in Jesus and asserted that mystical love for God made brotherly love mundane and irrelevant.

When this is recognized, attempts to discover an orderly structure for the Epistle will be abandoned and talk of a spiral argument will cease. But there is continuity of thought because the heretical affirmations are closely related to each other. As these provide the structure of the Epistle, there is a connection of thought between the various responses. But the connection does not provide a consistent development of argument. There is repetition and redevelopment in the face of these affirmations which reveal that the heretics themselves did not hold a unified position.

The seven affirmations are all of an anthropological nature. They assert the status and nature of the heretics. Their so-called theology was egocentric. Where relationship to God is spoken of, the self-affirmations by-pass the historical revelation in Jesus. All seven assertions ignore or deny the significance of the apostolic witness to Jesus. Two different positions appear to have been adopted by the heretics. Direct relationship with God was claimed without any reference to Christ. The second position allowed the heavenly Christ some significance, while refusing to acknowledge the authority of the apostolic witness to the historical Jesus. An examination of the affirmations will clarify the basic position of the heretics and indicate why they rejected the apostolic testimony.

1. 'If we say "We have fellowship with him" ...' (1.6)
The heretics claimed to have fellowship with God without reference to Christ. Fellowship was understood in terms of a subjective mystical experience lifting a person out of the tensions of historical existence, dispensing with the necessity of the historical revelation in Christ and the necessity of ethical conduct. To 'walk in the light' indicated, for them, the experience of mystical enlightenment (2.9). They thought that because they had a direct, immediate, experience with God, they did not need to worry about the way they lived.

2. 'If we say "We have no sin" ...' (1.8)
Those who claimed to have mystical fellowship with God considered themselves to be sinless as a consequence, and therefore they did not need Christ's redemptive work. The perfect have no need to be cleansed from sin. John asserts that those who make this claim have deceived themselves. The way to deal with sin is not to deny its existence but to confess it and to be cleansed through Jesus' saving death (1.7–9; 2.1f.).

3. 'If we say "We have not (ever) sinned" ...' (1.10)
This statement goes beyond the previous claim (in 1.8) to be sinless now, and asserts 'we have never sinned'. Here we are in touch with a Gnostic analysis of human nature. In some Gnostic systems men were divided into three groups:

(*a*) The men of 'matter' who cannot be saved;
(*b*) The men of 'the middle' who may be saved;
(*c*) The true Gnostics who would certainly be saved by virtue of their sinless spiritual natures.

It is the third group, who claimed to be saved by virtue of their sinless natures, that is in view in 1.10. Their claim shows that they have rejected the apostolic witness which would have led them to confess their sin.

4. 'He who says "I know him" ...' (2.4)
Who is it that the heretics claim to know, God or Christ?

> Bultmann claims that God is in view because the personal pronoun, *autos* (='he'), is always used to refer to God, while the personal pronoun *ekeinos* (='he'), is used of Christ. He disposes of 2.2,28, where *autos* is used to refer to Christ, by attributing these verses to the ecclesiastical redactor. This redaction theory is to be rejected. Nor would the readers have noticed such a fine distinction, had it existed. The evidence indicates that *ekeinos* is used for emphasis and only in the nominative case.

Verses 2 and 3 make clear that Christ is in view in 2.4. The heretics claimed mystical knowledge of 'Christ', possibly thinking of him as the heavenly Logos. Evidently the heretics were divided amongst themselves with regard to the object of mystical knowledge. But the difference is not as great as it may appear to be, because it is not the Jesus of history who is in view. It is the heavenly Christ, the Christ of experience. Hence they disregarded the historical revelation in which a commandment is laid on those who would know Jesus (3.23) (cf. Mark 12.28–34).

5. 'He who says "I abide in him" ...' (2.6)
The heretics' claim to abide in Christ is essentially the same as the claims to be in him (2.5) and to know him (2.4). It is to be

understood in terms of mystical abiding, ignoring the historical events of Jesus' life.

6. 'He who says "I am in the light" ...' (2.9)
The heretics claimed to be illuminated by supernatural knowledge, either by virtue of possessing a nature which partook of the essence of light, or through mystical experience. This claim also excluded the historical revelation in Jesus, with the ethical implication.

7. 'If anyone says "I love God" ...' (4.20)
The heretics claimed to love God, and because of this they denied the necessity of loving the brethren. The repeated command to love the brethren in 1 John is an indication that authentic Christianity was being threatened at the ethical level. This is related to the correct understanding of God's historical act in Christ. The heretics claimed to know God, dispensing with concern for the material world in their mystical love for God.

But John, unlike the Synoptic Gospels, does not speak of loving God in response to his love. The claim to love God was made by the heretics (4.20f.); and is put to the test of obedience to the command to love the brethren (4.21; 5.1–3) which Jesus gave (John 13.34). John interprets the heretics' claim to love God in terms of keeping his commandments (5.3) which in 3.23 are reduced to believing in Jesus and loving one another as Jesus commanded. The idea of loving God is brought into question by the following statements also:

(*a*) 'This is what love is—not that we loved God but that he loved us and sent his Son ...' (4.10).
(*b*) 'Beloved, if God loved us like this we ought also to love one another' (4.11). It is not said that we should love God in response to his love, as we might have expected.
(*c*) 'If we love one another God abides in us and his love is made perfect in us' (4.12). As we love one another, not, as we love God, as we might have expected.
(*d*) 'We love, because he first loved us' (4.19). It is not 'We love God ...', as we might have expected.

John does not speak of loving God directly. Love is directed towards the brother, as a consequence of believing in Jesus as witnessed to by the apostles (3.23; 5.1–4).

> 1 John 2.15–17 (as in the Gospel also) presents us with the antithesis of false and true loves. It is not that the heretics did not love. Their love was morally perverted and misdirected. They claimed to love God, but their words were empty of meaning because they did not take seriously the revelation or the commandments of God (3.16–18). In fact, their claim to love God is to be understood in terms of their own self-centredness, 'I love God' (4.20). This individualism is a rejection of the fellowship based on the revelation (1.5–7). It is the love of the darkness rather than the light. The revelation poses a moral question to man. It is the question of self-love or love of the neighbour. Paradoxically, those who claimed to have mystical love for God (some of them at least) were also guilty of what John calls love for the world (1 John 2.15f.). His command 'Do not love the world' invites us to think of God's love for the world (John 3.16). This comparison makes us aware of the different nature of the two loves. God's love for the world was expressed in his giving, 'God loved the world like this, he gave...'. God loved the sinful world in such a way as to make its transformation possible. But the love which John prohibits is man's attachment to the world whereby the sinful world controls man and conforms him to its image. The consequence is that man is controlled by 'lust', of the flesh (man's fallen being, not simply his physical nature), of the eyes (he wants to possess what he sees because that is reality to him), he is controlled by 'the pride of life', the desire to impress men with his own importance. This is 'to love the glory of men rather than the glory of God'. It is utterly opposed to the love which comes from God and consequently, like all things transient, it will vanish. But those who do the will of God abide for ever. For John, as for Paul, it is love alone that counts, triumphs over evil and endures for ever (1. Cor. 13).

John does not speak of loving God because for him 'God is love' and love comes as a gift from him. To speak of loving God in this context would involve a kind of spiritual narcissism. Love is grace, given freely. It would not be fitting to speak of man's response to God in such terms. The meaning of love as grace is given in the historical revelation (4.7–11).

The antithesis of 1 John 3.18 also draws our attention to the claims of the heretics. Their view is prohibited, while John commands his readers to follow another way. 'Little children, let us not love in word (*logō*) nor in the tongue (*tē glōssē*) but in work and truth.' John stresses the actual and faithful nature of love. His opponents could speak of love but they did not love the brethren. But what is love in the tongue? The fact that John's opponents were mystics of a Gnostic variety opens up the possibility that we have here a reference to an ecstatic tongue such as those known to Paul at Corinth. It is likely that the heretics claimed that in their ecstatic outpouring in the tongue they were pouring out love for God. As far as John was concerned, such a claim was meaningless. In his opposition to them he commanded, 'love in work and truth'. The concrete nature of this love is demonstrated in 1 John 3.16–17.

The heretics set themselves above the ordinary Christians with their claim to be in the possession of direct, immediate knowledge of God. Their claims led to uncertainty and a lack of assurance. John regarded those who made these exclusive claims as 'anti-Christ' (2.18ff.), and they are identified as those who denied that Jesus Christ had come in the flesh (4.2). Against this teaching, John asserts that all Christians have been anointed by the Holy One and as a consequence have knowledge (2.20). The anointing, related to baptism, involves faith in the apostolic testimony to Jesus (embodied in the rule of faith) and the presence of the Holy Spirit with all believers. The purpose of 1 John was to assure those who believed in Jesus that they had eternal life (5.13). The different background from which the Gospel comes is reflected in the stated purpose for which the Gospel was written (20.31). The aim of the Gospel was to bring Jewish Christians from a kind of faith in Jesus as a miracle-worker or Messiah to find in him the personal revelation of the eternal God. To have this authentic faith is to have life. 1 John was written to those whose faith had been confused and they now doubted their status. It was written in order that they might know their status. The Gospel faced the problem of Judaism. In 1 John the problem of paganism is faced, as the conclusion indicates, 'Little children, guard yourselves from idols' (5.21).

1 John was written to bring the assurance of faith to those who had been troubled by the heretical teachers. John uses a number of tests to expose the heretics and to confirm true knowledge. Some of the tests are to be recognized by their linguistic form, 'By this we know ...' (*en toutō ginōskomen* ...) 2.3,5; 3.24; 4.13; 5.2; 'By this you (plural) know ...' 4.2. The verb 'to know' is used in the present tense. The same form appears with the verb in the perfect tense in 3.16, drawing attention to the definitive revelation of love in the past, and in the future tense in 3.19 because it depends on the fulfilment of the condition of loving action. A similar form appears in 3.10 'By this are manifest ...' (*en toutō phanera estin* ...) and 4.9 'By this is manifest ...' (*en toutō ephanerōthē* ...). Another variation appears in 4.6 'By this we know ...' (*ek toutou* ...). The use of this form indicates a test on the basis of evidence which sometimes precedes the formula (as in 2.5; 3.19; 4.6); sometimes follows it (2.3; 3.10,16; 4.2,9); and sometimes seems to provide double evidence before and after the form (3.24; 4.13; 5.2).

The tests expose the heretics' false claims, to know God (Jesus) (2.3), to abide in God (Jesus) (3.24; 4.13), to be children of God (3.10; 5.2), to love God (3.16; 4.9f. and note 4.20), to be of the truth (3.19), to have the Spirit of God (4.2,6). The evidence used to falsify the claims is the confession of true faith and love for the brethren. Both have their foundation in the revelation of divine love in the historic event which has been known in the past (perfect tense) (3.16; 4.9–10). This event in the past is both the foundation of faith and the ground for loving action (4.11). Knowing is tested by keeping the commandments (2.3) thus exposing the false claims (2.4), and the commandments are understood in terms of believing in Jesus and loving one another (3.23). Abiding (2.5) involves keeping Jesus' word, 'Love one another as I have loved you' (John 15.12) and thus 'to walk as he walked' (2.6). While the form in 3.24 looks back to the test of 'keeping his commandments' as the evidence of abiding in him, it also looks forward to the evidence of the gift of the Spirit. Both aspects are related, because John understands love for the brethren and the confession of faith in Jesus as evidence of the presence of the Spirit of God. The heretics also appealed to the evidence of the Spirit, which they seem to have understood in terms of inspired ecstatic utterance (tongue, *glōssa*) (3.18). Against this, John stresses the active nature of love for the brethren and the manifestation of the Spirit of God in the confession of faith, 'Jesus Christ has come in the flesh'

(4.2,6; cf. 1 Cor. 12.2 and note the stress on love in 1 Cor. 13 in the context of the controversy about the place of inspired ecstatic utterance). While the evidence follows the form in 4.13, the nature of the manifestation of the Spirit has already been described. We return to the theme of love when love for the children of God is made the test for those who claim to love God (5.2 and note 4.20) as Dodd rightly stresses.

These tests demonstrate that the heretics had a faulty view of Christ and a faulty view of love. Thus the confession of true faith and active love for the brethren have become the tests which expose the heretics and provide the believers with the assurance of faith.

5 *The Response*

The response to the heretics was made at two levels, partly because they were divided into two groups. But even if this had not been the case, the response might have taken the same form because what most clearly distinguished the heretics from John was their doctrine of God. They were distinguished from each other by the place one of the groups gave to the heavenly Christ. His significance for them was determined by their doctrine of God and was quite different from John's assessment. In correcting their doctrine of God, John drew attention to the nature of God revealed in Christ (1 John 5.20–21). This method had the effect of fighting on two levels at the same time. But it is also the way in which the theme of revelation is dealt with in the Gospel (John 17.3). In the Gospel, in the context of Judaism, the controversy concerns the nature of revelation (John 1.14–18, etc.). In 1 John, in the context of paganism, the controversy concerns the nature of God and of religious experience. In the Gospel, John argues that Jesus is the revelation, whereas in 1 John he argues that God is known only in his revelation and that true religious experience arises from the acceptance of that revelation.

The two most significant statements in 1 John, 'God is light' (1.5), and 'God is love' (4.8,16) are both statements about God and are set in contexts which indicate that the meaning of light and love is determined by the nature of the revelation in Jesus. Because 'God is light' he is not the source of the darkness, 'there is no darkness in him at all'. In the Gospel, light was a symbol for the revelation. This statement asserts that God is a God who reveals himself and that there is nothing in him that is contrary to his revelation. Light also indicates something about the character of God and the nature of the revelation (John 3.19ff.; 1 John 2.9ff.). Light excludes hatred and involves love.

The message that 'God is light' is the essence of the apostolic witness to the Word of Life. 1 John 1.1–4 emphasizes the eye-witness basis of the apostolic testimony to the revelation of God in Jesus. The purpose of the open announcement of this testimony was that the hearers might have fellowship with the eye-witnesses and, through their testimony, with the Father and the Son to whom they bore witness. In 1.5ff. the terms of the announcement were modified, perhaps because the heretics claimed to be 'in the light' (2.9). For them this meant 'to have fellowship with God'. But fellowship with God was only possible through walking in the light of the revelation in Jesus, and therefore only in fellowship with the eye-witnesses. The apostolic witness to Jesus' death raised the problem of man's sinfulness in such a way that it could only be dealt with by confessing it and relying on God's loving kindness, revealed in Jesus, for forgiveness.

The meaning of love is given definitively in the statement 'God is love'. But that would have been an empty definition, had the meaning not been demonstrated in the event in which God revealed what his love was like (1 John 4.7ff., especially 4.9). The sending of Jesus revealed God's self-giving love, in that Jesus came to give life to the world by the giving of his own life (2.2; 4.10); which in some way has the power to cleanse man from sin (1.7), bringing forgiveness to those who respond to the revelation of God's love (1.9). That 'God is love' in this sense was revealed in the life and especially the death of Jesus, as witnessed to by the apostles.

All the claims of the heretics were subjected to two closely related tests. The claims to know God were tested by the standard of the apostolic testimony to Jesus. 'He who knows God hears us ...' (4.6). Those who reject the apostolic testimony are false prophets, the antichrist, inspired by the spirit of error, (4.1,3,6). The apostolic testimony of the eye-witnesses inspired by the Spirit of God (John 15.26f.) is expressed in the confession that Jesus Christ has come in the flesh (4.2). Acceptance of this testimony makes the life of Jesus determinative for faith and life. His words or commands are to be obeyed (2.4) and his example is to be followed (2.6). This test rests on the acceptance of the fact that God is known in Jesus (2.23,24; 5.20) and leads naturally on to the second test.

If the first test was the test of a sound faith, the second test is the test of right conduct. In the revelation in Jesus the love of God is made known. The claim to know God can be tested by the way a person lives. Knowledge of God, who is light, leads to walking in the light (1.5ff.) and this is understood in terms of loving the brethren as God loved us (2.9f.). The heretics' claims were refuted by their conduct (3.6). Because the life given through the coming of Jesus was from God, those who failed to love the brethren revealed that they were abiding in death (3.14–15). The person who does not love does not know God (4.7,8) because the knowledge of God ought to lead men to be like him (4.11). Hence the command to love the brethren is laid upon those who know the love of God in Jesus.

The essence of the whole matter is summed up in 1 John 3.23, where all the commandments are reduced to: 'Believe in the name of his Son Jesus Christ and love one another as he [Jesus] gave you commandment' (John 13.34). The command to love depends on acceptance of the apostolic witness to Jesus, for it is to be, as Jesus said, 'Love one another as I have loved you'. Hence the command to love is laid only upon those who accept the apostolic testimony to Jesus. While the threat of the heresy was at the ethical level, it could only be overcome by asserting the authority of the apostolic witness.

PART FOUR

Conclusion

Conclusion

This study has produced certain conclusions which seem to hang together consistently. The Gospel of John is best understood against a Jewish background that has been profoundly influenced by the Old Testament. But it is the Old Testament as it was interpreted in the first century of the Christian era. The critical importance of the Qumran texts is obvious, being the only known corpus of Palestinian Jewish literature from this period. The affinity that the Gospel shows with this corpus has been one of the outstanding discoveries of New Testament scholarship in the past thirty years. But John cannot be understood simply against the background of Qumran or the Judaism of the first century as a whole. Time and again the interpreter is forced to consider John's relation to primitive Christianity as a whole and to Paul and the Synoptic tradition in particular. In John there is a unique blending of the gospel tradition with the primitive Christian interpretation of that material and its implications. Of course the Synoptic Gospels are also interpretation, but John goes further. Not only this, he develops the implications of the gospel tradition, the meaning of faith, the experience of eternal life and freedom as Paul does. But, unlike Paul, he has embedded this development in the gospel tradition concerning Jesus, thus safeguarding the unity of the Jesus of history and the Christ of faith in a manner which is not explicitly spelt out by Paul or any other writer in the New Testament.

The Gospel material presupposes a Jewish situation. It is the expression of the gospel in a Jewish Christian community where pressure was brought to bear by the Jews to dissuade individuals from believing and to cause believers to compromise their faith. The threat of excommunication became a fearful weapon in these circumstances. From the Christian point of view, light is shed on this situation from the known conflict between Paul and the Jews and the Judaizers, especially from his letters, Galatians, 1 and

2 Corinthians and Romans, as well as the book of Acts.

Against the unbelieving Jews and the Judaizers with a deficient view of Christ, John had to assert the place of Jesus in salvation history. If consistent existential interpretation involves the rejection of the salvation history perspective, then ultimately it can only do violence to the meaning intended by John. For him the Jewish perspective is no symbol, it is historically vital for understanding the significance of Jesus. For this reason John is concerned to talk of Jesus in terms of the revelation of God in him and the relation of this revelation to creation and the Old Testament. The latter relation is one of the major themes of the Gospel. This is not surprising if the Gospel developed in a Jewish situation. In the Gospel, the stress is on the fact that it was the Word who became flesh. None of the opponents of Jesus suggest that he was not a man. Again and again the Jews deny that God is known in him, they deny that God is at work in him, they charge him with blasphemy for claiming to be one with God. In the Jewish situation the christological question was at stake and John asserted that Jesus was the unique Son of God, through whom alone God is known and through whom alone man may come to God.

The truth about Jesus could only be known by faith, believing in him or initially by believing in his words or his works. Those who honestly persist in this way are assured that they will come to believe authentically. Believing is the most dominant motif in the Gospel, which was written in order that 'you may believe' in this authentic sense.

The significance of believing in this way, which arises out of the nature of the revelation in Jesus, is interpreted again in the Jewish situation. The binding nature of Judaism is broken for the believer, who is bound only to Jesus and as a consequence of this, to his brother also. While believing involves the intellectual acceptance of Jesus as the unique Son of God, it includes also, as a matter of course, obedience to the Son of God.

The truth about Jesus could be known only by faith, and this believing was dependent on the resurrection of Jesus and the coming of the Paraclete. The Gospel is emphatic that believing involves knowledge of the Jesus of history, of his death and also of his resurrection. The significance of the resurrection is emphasized by the fact that when 'the beloved disciple' saw the empty tomb, he believed. Paul said that Jesus was 'declared to be Son of God by a mighty act, according to the Holy Spirit, in his resurrection from among the dead' (Rom. 1.4). John develops this theme. True faith in Jesus was based on believing eye-witness experience of the risen Jesus, illuminated by the teaching and reminding activity of the Spirit of Truth, whose primary task was to bring understanding of Jesus' place in the history of salvation. Thus it was only to those who believed that Jesus appeared after his resurrection, and to whom the Paraclete came.

John was also concerned with the question of the continuation of the revelation after Jesus' departure. The answer is given in terms of the coming of the Paraclete and the believing witness of the apostles. The eye-witnesses of Jesus' life, death and resurrection, were bound to Jesus' Word, which he had given them (his total revelation), illuminated by the Paraclete. Down through the ages, believers would be bound to Jesus through the inspired understanding given by the original eye-witnesses. If perhaps many of these had died before John wrote, we have all the more reason for supposing that he conceived of his Gospel as the expression of this inspired apostolic witness in writing. If we ask the question about apostolic succession of authority, John would answer in terms of his Gospel, or to generalize, we would say that the New Testament is the successor to the authority of the apostles.

If these conclusions are correct, we would expect that any Jewish Christian community accepting them would soon be ostracized from Judaism. John emphasizes the necessity of open witness to and confession of Jesus. Acceptance of this could only lead to a break with Judaism and an openness to gentile mission. After A.D. 70 there was an increasingly serious rift between Judaism and Christianity. The actual publication of John takes account of this situation and certain minor modifications have been made to a Gospel that is basically Jewish in character. The significance of the material can only be properly understood against the background of the problems of the early Jewish Christians. But by publication date, gentiles were already entering this

Christian community, as the explanation of Jewish customs indicates. These explanations may have been added with the appendix, chapter 21.

In this new situation this Jewish Gospel had a great relevance. It asserts the significance of the Old Testament read from the perspective of Christ (salvation history). It sets out the nature of apostolic authority and witness. Both aspects were to prove to be extremely important for the Church down through the ages.

Apparently the Gospel proved to be attractive to pagan 'converts'. This is not surprising, as the language of John, like that of the Qumran texts, had developed under the impact of Hellenism. John's language was clear and intelligible within the context of the Judaeo–Christian tradition (salvation history), but was open to all kinds of abuse when understood from the perspective of individualistic and subjective religious experience. The crisis of this new way of understanding is encountered by John in his first letter. What was now at stake was not the divine Sonship of Jesus but his actual humanity; not the reality of revelation in him but its historical nature. The change of emphasis indicates the change of context from Judaism to paganism. Thus 1 John concludes (in a manner unnecessary in Judaism) 'Little children, guard yourselves from idols'. The stress is no longer on believing (as in the Gospel), though the confession of the real humanity of Jesus is crucial now. The stress is now on the historical nature of the revelation and its ethical implications. True religious experience is not 'my subjective relation to or with God'. It is the awareness and acceptance of the love of God revealed in the life and death of Jesus, who is known to be the Son of God, and the willingness to live in the light of his love. In this new situation, it is the true nature of the divine love revealed in history that is central. It is the implication of this love for the believer that is emphasized. This historical revelation is what is known in the apostolic witness. John claims authority for this witness and interprets it in terms of the revelation of the love of God in history, the call to accept this love and to live in the light of it. True religious experience arises from the apostolic witness and may be tested by it.

If the Gospel stands over against Jewish legalism, asserting the primacy of Jesus in salvation history, then 1 John stands over against pagan mysticism, asserting the primacy of the apostolic witness to Jesus as the source and test of all true religious experience. Ultimately John was fighting on these two fronts, as Paul had, against legalism in Galatians and against mysticism in 1 Corinthians. But for Paul, both battles were often carried on simultaneously precisely because of his involvement in gentile mission. For John they appear to have been successive conflicts because the pagan challenge came only after the break with Judaism had forced the apostle, who saw his mission in terms of Judaism (Gal. 2.9), to take account of the pagan response. While Paul carried on his mission to the gentiles and attempted at the same time to maintain unity with the Jewish Christians and contact with Judaism in general, John's contact with pagan piety come only after the break from Judaism. Paul's conflict with Judaism and the Judaizers primarily concerned the basis for the admission of gentiles to the Church, while the conflict portrayed in the Gospel concerned Christology. Faith in Jesus as the unique Son of God in Johannine terms, was blasphemous to Judaism. Of course the christological conflict was also present for Paul. But the conflict over the question of the gentiles is much more prominent, whereas for John, the basis of gentile admission is not in dispute. What is in dispute is the question of the significance and authority of Jesus, and this dispute is carried on in terms of Jesus' relation to Judaism. This difference between Paul and John points to the basic gentile situation of the Pauline mission and the Jewish situation which forms the background of John's Gospel.

The theology of the Gospel is developed in such a manner as to show that faith in Jesus involves the believer in Jesus' mission. While it is true that the Gospel has a world perspective of mission, it is the Jewish mission in particular that is in focus. It is the situation of the Jewish believer that concerns John. The world mission perspective is the background to the concern for the Jewish mission in particular. With the break from Judaism, perhaps the background perspective has become more important to the reader than the actual theme John had in view, just as John's emphasis on salvation history and the place of the eye-witnesses took on a new significance in the pagan environment against which 1 John was written.

The Church down through the ages has been plagued by legalism and mysticism. If Paul and John are right, neither of these two approaches to God is open to authentic Christian faith. Both are excluded by the primacy of the revelation in Christ, understood in the context of salvation history and witnessed to by the apostles. This is the ground and test of all authentic religious experience. John gives a clearer and more consistent rejection of the threat of mysticism than Paul because of the manner in which the Jesus of history and the Christ of faith are united in the Gospel. It is not that this differs from the Pauline view. It is simply that Paul has not given a clear treatment of this aspect. John's detailed treatment of the role of the Spirit in the community of believers is most important, because current mystical tendencies, like those in second-century Gnosticism, concentrate on the experience of the Spirit. But the Spirit maintains the primacy of the revelation in Christ in the context of salvation history. Here the foundation is laid for understanding Christian experience in terms of the true confession of faith and the life of love.

Unlike the Synoptic Gospels and the Old Testament, John does not speak of man's response to God in terms of love (apart from love for one another). He understood love as the motivation of undeserved action, God's love for the world. The disciple's love for the brother was not to be based on any consideration of whether that love was deserved or not. Jesus' command was 'love one another in the same manner as I have loved you'.

John also differs from the Old Testament in his use of 'believe'. In the Old Testament, both love and faithfulness could be used equally of God's activity towards man and man's response to God. For John, believing is man's proper response to God's revelation and love becomes the key description of God's initiative in relation to the world. Even where love for Jesus is spoken of, it is interpreted in the sense of the Old Testament tradition of obedience. The Gospel does not indicate that these two different ways of speaking of love raise any problem.

In 1 John, the heretics' claim to love God was put forward as an alternative to keeping the commandments, and in particular, as an alternative to love for the brethren. They interpreted love for God in the context of mysticism rather than the Old Testament. In this situation John insisted that, where love for God was spoken of, it should be interpreted as obedience to his commands. In fact, he puts in question the propriety of speaking of love for God at all. Certainly his own preference was to speak of believing in Jesus and loving one another.

Bibliography and Indexes

Select Bibliography

More extensive bibliographies are to be found in the commentaries on the Gospel by R. E. Brown, B. Lindars, and Rudolf Schnackenburg, and on the Epistles by Rudolf Bultmann and Rudolf Schnackenburg. Much valuable information is to be gained from the various New Testament introductions and from the New Testament theologies by Rudolph Bultmann, *Theology of the New Testament*, 2 vols, S.C.M. 1965-71; Hans Conzelmann, *Outline of the Theology of the New Testament*, S.C.M. 1969; W. G. Kummell, *Theology of the New Testament*, S.C.M. 1974.

COMMENTARIES ON THE FOURTH GOSPEL

(* indicates the most important and † the best of the more concise publications)

*Barrett, C. K., *The Gospel According to St John*. S.P.C.K. 1955.

*Brown, R. E., *The Gospel According to John*, 2 vols. Doubleday 1966.

*Bultmann, R., *The Gospel of John*. Blackwell 1971.

Fenton, J. C., *The Gospel According to John*. Oxford 1970.

Hoskyns, E. C., *The Fourth Gospel*. Faber & Faber 1947.

†Howard, W. F., *John* (*Interpreter's Bible* vol. 8). Abingdon 1952.

Lightfoot, R. H., *St John's Gospel*. Oxford 1956.

*Lindars, B., *The Gospel of John*. Oliphants 1972.

Marsh, J., *The Gospel of St John*. Pelican 1968.

Morris, L., *The Gospel of John*. Marshall, Morgan & Scott 1972.

Richardson, A., *St John*. S.C.M. 1959.

Sanders, J. N. and Mastin, B. A., *The Gospel According to St John*. Black 1968.

Schnackenburg, R., *The Gospel According to St John*, vol. 1. Burns & Oates 1968.

Tasker, R. V. G., *John*. I.V.P. 1960.

Westcott, B. F., *St John*. James Clarke 1958.

COMMENTARIES ON THE JOHANNINE EPISTLES

*Brooke, A. E., A *Critical and Exegetical Commentary on the Johannine Epistles*. T. & T. Clark 1912.

*Bultmann, R., *The Johannine Epistles*. Fortress Press 1973.

*†Dodd, C. H., *The Johannine Epistles*. Hodder & Stoughton 1946.

†Houlden, J. L., A *Commentary on the Johannine Epistles*. Black 1973.

Law, R., *The Tests of Life*. T. & T. Clark 1909.

Stott, J. R. W., *Epistles of John*. Tyndale Press 1964.

Westcott, B. F., *The Epistles of St John*. Abingdon 1966.

Wilder, A. N., *The Epistles of John* (*Interpreter's Bible*, vol. 12). Abingdon 1957.

STUDIES ON THE BACKGROUND TO THE GOSPEL AND EPISTLES

The commentaries and introductions normally treat this subject.

1. GENERAL BACKGROUND

Barrett, C. K., *The New Testament Background: Selected Documents*. S.P.C.K. 1956.

Bultmann, R., *Primitive Christianity in its Contemporary Setting*. Fontana 1956.

*Dodd, C. H., *Interpretation of the Fourth Gospel*. C.U.P. 1953.

2. CONCERNING GNOSTICISM

Foerster, W., *Gnosis I*. Oxford 1972.

†Grant, R. M., *Gnosticism: An Anthology*. Collins 1961.

—, *Gnosticism and Early Christianity*. Columbia 1967.

Hardt, R., *Gnosis*. Brill 1971.

Jonas, H., *The Gnostic Religion*. Beacon Press 1958.

*Wilson, R. McL., ed., *New Testament Apocrypha*, 2 vols., Lutterworth 1963, 1965.

—, *Gnosis and the New Testament*. Blackwell 1968.

—, *The Gnostic Problem*. Mowbrays 1958.

†Yamauchi, E., *Pre-Christian Gnosticism*. Tyndale Press 1973.

3. CONCERNING QUMRAN

Black, M., *The Dead Sea Scrolls and Christian Doctrine*. Athlone Press 1966.

*Charlesworth, J. H., ed., *John and Qumran*. Geoffrey Chapman 1972.

*Vermès, G., *The Dead Sea Scrolls in English*. Penguin 1962.

4. CONCERNING JOHN AND JUDAISM

*Barrett, C. K., *The Gospel of John and Judaism*. S.P.C.K. 1975.

Borgen, P., *Bread from Heaven*. Brill 1965.

Guilding, A., *The Fourth Gospel and Jewish Worship*. London 1960.

*Martyn, J. L., *History and Theology in the Fourth Gospel*. Harper & Row 1968.

Meeks, W. A., *The Prophet-King*. Leiden 1967.

SURVEYS OF JOHANNINE STUDIES

Fuller, R. H., *The New Testament in Current Study* (S.C.M. 1963), pp. 114-44.

Howard, W. F. and Barrett, C. K., *The Fourth Gospel in Recent Criticism and Interpretation*. Epworth 1955.

Neill, S., *The Interpretation of the New Testament 1861-1961* (O.U.P. 1966), pp. 308-24.

JOHN AND THE EARLY CHURCH

Pagelis, E. H., *The Johannine Gospel in Gnostic Exegesis*. Abingdon 1973.

Sanders, J. N., *The Fourth Gospel in the Early Church*. C.U.P. 1943.

Wiles, M. F., *The Spiritual Gospel*. C.U.P. 1960.

SOURCES AND HISTORICITY OF JOHN

*Dodd, C. H., *Historical Tradition in the Fourth Gospel*. C.U.P. 1963.

Fortna, R., *The Gospel of Signs*. C.U.P. 1970.

Freed, E. G., *Old Testament Quotations in the Gospel of John*. Brill 1965.

Higgins, A. J. B., *The Historicity of the Fourth Gospel*. Lutterworth 1960.

Nicol, W., *The Semeia in the Fourth Gospel*. Brill 1972.

*Smith, D. M., *The Composition and Order of the Fourth Gospel*. Yale 1965.

JOHANNINE THEOLOGY

Valuable discussions are to be found in many of the works already listed.

Barrett, C. K., *New Testament Essays* (S.P.C.K. 1972), pp. 27-69.

Batey, R., *New Testament Issues* (S.C.M. 1970), pp. 191-241.

Boice, J. M., *Witness and Revelation in the Gospel of John*. Paternoster 1970.

Borsch, F. H., *The Son of Man in Myth and History* (S.C.M. 1967), especially pp. 257-313.

Bultmann, R., *Theology of the New Testament*, vol. 2, S.C.M. 1955.

Corell, A., *Consumatum Est*. S.P.C.K. 1958.

Cross, F. L., *Studies in the Fourth Gospel*. Mowbray 1957.

Cullman, O., *Salvation in History* (S.C.M. 1967), pp. 268-91.

Davey, J. E., *The Jesus of St John*. Lutterworth 1958.

*Dodd, C. H., *Interpretation of the Fourth Gospel*. C.U.P. 1953.

Glasson, T. F., *Moses in the Fourth Gospel*. S.C.M. 1963.

Higgins, A. J. B., *The Words of Jesus According to St John*. John Rylands Library 1967.

Holwerda, D. E., *The Holy Spirit and Eschatology in the Gospel of John*. Kampen, J. H. Kok, 1959.

*†Howard, W. F., *Christianity According to St John*. Duckworth 1943.

Hunter, A. M., *According to John*. S.C.M. 1968.

*Johnston, G., *The Spirit-Paraclete in the Gospel of John*. C.U.P 1970.

Käsemann, E., *Jesus Means Freedom* (S.C.M. 1969), pp. 144-53

—, *The Testament of Jesus*. S.C.M. 1968.

Lee, F. K., *The Religious Thought of St John*. S.P.C.K. 1950

*Manson, T. W., *On Paul and John* (S.C.M. 1963), pp. 85-160

Morris, L., *Studies in the Fourth Gospel*. Paternoster 1969.

Mussner, F., *The Historical Jesus in the Gospel of St John.* Burns & Oates 1966.

Nygren, A., *Agape and Eros.* S.P.C.K. 1932.

Pollard, T. E., *Johannine Christology and the Early Church.* C.U.P. 1970.

Robinson, J. A. T., *Twelve New Testament Studies.* S.C.M. 1962.

Sanders, J. T., *The New Testament Christological Hymns* (C.U.P. 1971), pp. 29-57.

Sidebottom, E. M., *The Christ of the Fourth Gospel.* S.P.C.K. 1961.

Smalley, S., *New Light on the Fourth Gospel* (Tyndale Bulletin 17, 1966), pp. 35-62.

No bibliography of journal articles is given here in spite of the fact that the significance of some of these has not been given expression in the commentaries and monographs listed above. But bibliographies to journal articles are available in some of the major commentaries as indicated above. Finally, attention should be drawn to a work of a category and significance all on its own.

Friedrich, G., and Kittel, G., *Theological Dictionary of the New Testament*, 9 vols, tr. G. W. Bromiley. Eerdmans 1964-74.

This work contains, among other things, a mine of information about the background, use, meaning, and significance of the Johannine theological vocabulary.

Reference needs to be made to one commentary on the Johannine Epistles written in German because there is no contemporary work of a similar scope in the English language.

Schnackenburg, R., *Die Johannesbriefe.* Herder 1963.

Index of Names and Subjects

Index of Biblical References

INDEX OF BIBLICAL REFERENCES

INDEX OF BIBLICAL REFERENCES

INDEX OF BIBLICAL REFERENCES